THE GENTLE ART of VERBAL SELF-DEFENSE

Suzette Haden Elgin

REVISED & UPDATED

THE GENTLE ART of VERBAL SELF-DEFENSE

Suzette Haden Elgin

FALL RIVER PRESS

Book Design by MELISSA CHANG/HSU + ASSOCIATES

FALL RIVER PRESS
122 Fifth Avenue
New York, NY 10011

ISBN: 978-1-4351-1342-8

Printed and bound in the UNITED STATES OF AMERICA

10 9 8 7 6 5 4 3 2 1

CONTENTS

Acknowledgments

The list of people I owe thanks to is very long. It includes all those who have worked with me over the years as my students, my clients, my trainers, and as participants in my workshops and seminars; they have been my continual and always reliable source of information about communication in the real world. My thanks go also to all my readers, for the constant (and indispensable) flow of letters and materials that they send me, and for the answers they provide to my endless questions.

Thanks are owed to...

Linguist **Leonard Newmark**, who taught me everything I know about how to make people want to learn and how to convince them to come eagerly to the learning experience.

To linguist **John Grinder**, who helped me at the very beginning of my work with the Gentle Art system, especially when I was struggling to fight my way through tangled thickets of scientific jargon and gibberish.

To Navajo linguist and educator **Caroline (Kathy) Begaye Bemore**, who taught me how English works by helping me study it through the lens of Navajo.

To my daughter and colleague **Rebecca Haden**, who has always been ready with encouragement and support, and whose usefully different ways of perceiving this world have so often made it possible for me to step outside the frame I would otherwise have been trapped in, so that I could see and hear and feel with more clarity and more skill.

To my literary agent **Jeff McCartney**, who is always there for me with patient help and guidance.

To attorney and mediator **Stephen Marsh**, who for decades has gone far beyond the call of duty in helping me struggle against the blight of hostile language.

To my editors, **Betsy Beier**, **Rachel Federman**, and **Suzanne Fass**, who have led me through the writing of this book with unfailing patience and courtesy; I am especially indebted to Rachel Federman for always posing exactly the right questions.

I owe special thanks to all my readers and commenters at Live Journal, who have again and again volunteered their time and energy to the often tedious task of discussing bits and pieces of verbal self-defense with me, and who have been lavishly generous with their knowledge about hostile language in today's new electronic communications media.

I am deeply grateful to my long-suffering husband, **George Elgin**, and to all our children and grandchildren, who have provided me with many of the best of my examples and dialogues, together with daily opportunities to hone my verbal self-defense skills.

My work would have been impossible without that of many others whose wisdom I have been able to call upon. I am especially indebted to **Paul Watzlawick**, **Virginia Satir**, **Edward T. Hall**, **George Miller**, **Noam Chomsky**, **Ronald Langacker**, **Cheris Kramarae**, and **Sally McConnell-Ginet**.

I alone am responsible for any errors or omissions.

If you have comments about this book, questions to ask, or information you would like to share with me, I would be pleased to hear from you.

Suzette Haden Elgin, PhD
P. O. Box 1137
Huntsville, AR 72740-1137

Preface to the New Edition

When I wrote the first edition of this book in 1979, we were living in a world very different from the one we live in today. At that time, the concept of an interconnected global community, where people could be in actual contact with others around the clock even if they were nowhere near a computer, was science fiction. There were no PDAs; there were no cell phones. The option that every teenager has available today—the option of never being truly alone—didn't exist. There was no need for me to put any material about e-mail, or any other form of e-language, in that first edition.

Hostile language, and especially the hostile language associated with all the "-isms" that still plague us today—elitism, sexism, racism, classism, ageism, and more—was also very different. It was far more open and overt in the late 70s than it is today. My department chairman felt perfectly comfortable telling me that the rest of the faculty had been willing to "humor me temporarily" about a disagreement. Furthermore, my chairman was baffled when I took that statement as an insult. He wasn't faking, he was being absolutely honest; in that 1979 world, he didn't perceive what he'd said to me as insulting in any way. Men routinely referred to their wives as "the little woman" and to female employees as "my girls," and no one found that surprising.

The world has changed. The language environment has changed (and I see nothing to make me feel that it has grown less hostile or less toxic). The gaps separating the various generations are, in my opinion, wider and deeper now than they've ever been in our history. Today's children literally cannot imagine the world of their grandparents and great-grandparents. That world is as foreign to them as the world in traditional fairy tales. And it works both ways: the elders have no understanding of the younger generations' world, either.

Perhaps most astonishing of all is the blazing speed with which this revolution has taken place. It shows no signs of slowing down, and the uncertainty about tomorrow has a size and scope now that none of us, whatever our age, could ever have imagined in the late 1970s. Today we have no idea what our world, in every sense of the word "world," is going to be like in a future that is now rapidly bearing down on us.

It's time for a new version of this book, revised and updated for today's world, no question about it. I'm grateful to Fall River Press for being willing to let me write that new edition.

Suzette Haden Elgin

Introduction

"It's only talk, right?"

"It's only semantics, right?"

"Sticks and stones will break your bones, but words will never hurt you!"

Right?

Wrong. Quite wrong.

The idea that hostile language can't hurt you because it's "only words" has been part of our cultural consensus for generations. It continues to be supported by scholars and experts who write books and teach courses claiming that people who are hurt by hostile language are neurotic—or worse. It continues to be something that parents teach their children. It turns up in negative statements like "She can't take a joke" and "He has no sense of humor" and "She's always getting her poor little feelings hurt" and "He's forever making mountains out of molehills." Summed up, the claim is that this is what happens in the real world:

1. Somebody says something hurtful to you.

2. You say to yourself, "That hurt!"

3. You think, "I'm wrong. Words can't hurt me."

4. You think all you have to do to put an end to being hurt is stop saying dumb things like "That hurt!" to yourself.

That list contains a small thread of truth. It's true that you can torture yourself with words very effectively if you work at it hard enough. You can go over and over the hostile words that were said to you. You can make a kind of tape recording in your head, so it's easy to replay the scene. You can spend large chunks of your time doing these things and hurt yourself a lot. But an extreme reaction like that is different from a simple honest reaction of pain in response to verbal abuse.

We know a great deal more about the effects of hostile language today than we knew in the past, much of it learned only recently. We know beyond all question that, like sticks and stones, words can hurt you badly. So badly that you need to know a system for defending yourself against them. That system—the Gentle Art of Verbal Self-Defense—is the subject of this book.

WHY YOU NEED TO KNOW VERBAL SELF-DEFENSE

People who are skilled in verbal self-defense benefit from their skills; the payoff for learning those skills is very high. There are three major reasons why learning verbal self-defense can be the most important step you take in your life. Let's look at them one at a time.

The Link Between
Verbal Violence and Physical Violence

The reason we don't have enough money to do the things we want and need to do is that we spend so much of our money dealing with physical violence and its consequences. We spend enormous sums on law enforcement, on jails and prisons, on the legal system and the courts, on security, on insurance, on preventing and dealing with domestic violence, on the uninsured medical costs of violent criminals and their victims. We all know how those costs keep growing, and how out of control they are.

But the "words can't hurt you" idea keeps us from noticing the obvious: that almost all physical violence starts as verbal violence—as hostile language. Sane people don't just walk up to other people and start hitting. First there is an exchange of hostile words; then the physical violence starts. Even in cases where someone walks into their school or church or workplace and starts shooting, there is almost always a history of hostile language leading up to that tragic final event.

Once violence becomes physical, we need professionals to deal with it—police officers and emergency personnel and medical experts; it's out of our hands. But while the violence is still "only words," every person who speaks a language can learn how to deal with it and how to keep it from escalating into physical violence. To get a handle on physical violence and stop wasting our resources on it, we need to tackle it where it starts, while it's still hostile language. That means learning verbal self-defense. It means learning how to establish and maintain a language environment in which hostile language is very rare; it means learning how to deal with hostile language effectively and efficiently when it truly cannot be avoided.

The Link Between Language and Health

Sometimes things that seem obvious and self-evident—like the flatness of the Earth when you look at it as you're driving through Illinois—are only illusions. Sometimes we aren't able to see that, because we don't have the right technology for working with the data. The link between language and health is like that. Only recently have we been able to get a good, clear look at that link and begin to understand what it means.

We used to have to study medical histories with paper and pen and calculator, and that gave us one picture—one very limited picture—of what was going on. Today, the powerful computers that can show us hundreds of thousands of medical histories over the course of decades give us a very *different* picture: they show us that over time, hostile language maims and kills just like sticks and stones and knives and guns maim and kill. We couldn't see that before, because we didn't have enough data. Now we can see it, and the data tell us that hostile language is perhaps the most dangerous of all "risk factors." More dangerous than obesity, more dangerous than smoking, more dangerous than high cholesterol, more dangerous than all those things we put so much effort into avoiding. The information that appears when you look at enough medical data to see long-term patterns tells us unambiguously that people who are chronically exposed to hostile language get sick more often, are injured more often, take longer to recover from illness and injury, and die younger.

And there's more, thanks to those same powerful computers. We now know that hostile language isn't dangerous just to those who are its target. It's also dangerous to the person dishing it out, and it's dangerous to innocent bystanders who can't avoid it. That changes things dramatically. That means that it's just as important for verbal abusers to learn how to communicate without hostile language as it is for verbal targets to learn how to defend themselves against their attackers. Hostile language is toxic; to keep it out of your life, you need to learn verbal self-defense.

The Link Between Language and Success in Today's World

There was a time when most people got jobs and stayed in them for many years; there was a time when most people worked for one company, maybe two, until they retired. Individuals might move up through the ranks over time, but the company was like family; everybody knew everybody else.

In those days there was plenty of time for people to get used to one another at work. When new people were hired, somebody would fill them in. Like this:

> **"Don't pay any attention to the things Jack says; he's really a nice guy, and he doesn't mean to sound like such a jerk."**

> **"Just ignore Amanda when she starts mouthing off, she doesn't mean any of it."**

> **"Don't let the way Henderson talks fool you—he sounds stupid, but he's really one of the smartest guys in the company."**

As long as you showed up every day for work and did your best, you could assume that you'd get ahead, even if your communication skills were poor.

That has now changed dramatically. Now people change jobs, even change their whole careers, at a moment's notice. Within a single job, they move from project to project, and from team to team. To succeed today you need to be able to make a good impression immediately, establish instant rapport, and communicate successfully with people you've only just met. The luxury of lead time for gradually adjusting to others in your workplace has disappeared. Poor communication skills today are a serious barrier to success.

You may feel that this doesn't matter to you personally. You may already have succeeded in your chosen field; you may already have climbed high enough on the ladder. But if you have children and/or grandchildren, I assure you that it still does matter. If you want a tranquil retirement, free of children and grandchildren desperate for your help because they can't earn their own livings in today's world, you need to learn verbal self-defense so that you can make sure *their* language skills are topnotch.

Developing your verbal self-defense skills is in your own best interest, and it will repay your investment of learning time and energy many times over. To learn verbal self-defense, you need only your fluency in your native language, your common sense— and this book. The book will teach you the following things:

1. How to recognize patterns of verbal abuse in your own speech, so that you can stop using them

2. How to recognize verbal target patterns in your own language behavior, so that you can stop using them

3. How to recognize patterns of verbal abuse in the language behavior of others, so that you will be aware of them and know where the sources of contamination in your own language environment are

4. How to use a set of verbal self-defense techniques that will let you either defuse verbal attacks in advance and avoid hostility, or respond to them effectively when the confrontation cannot be avoided

5. How to use patterns of language that will improve the way others perceive you when that perception is based on your language behavior

6. How to eliminate patterns of language behavior that detract from the perception others have of you

⑦ How to interact verbally and nonverbally with others in such a way that your communication is more efficient and more satisfactory

It's not true that these accomplishments are limited to people with advanced degrees in communication, language arts, and linguistics, or to people "born with a silver tongue in their mouths." You are equipped to do all these things, no matter what your present level of expertise may be, simply because you are a native speaker of your language.

Welcome to the Gentle Art of Verbal Self-Defense.

1

The Four Basic Principles

For every person in this society who is suffering physical abuse, there are hundreds suffering the effects of verbal violence. For every person who just got a fist in the face, there are hundreds who just took a verbal blow to the gut. And there are major differences between these two kinds of injury.

The physical attack is at least obvious and unmistakable; when someone slugs you physically, you can call the police. The physical attack hurts horribly and leaves a mark, but it's usually over fast, and the mark is evidence in your favor and against your attacker.

Verbal violence is a very different matter. Except in rare cases—for example, when someone lies about you publicly before witnesses and can be charged with slander—there's no agency that you can call for help. The pain of verbal abuse goes deep into the self and festers there, but because nothing shows on the surface it will not win you even sympathy, much less actual assistance.

Worst of all, verbal violence all too often goes unrecognized, except at a level that you yourself cannot even understand. You know that you're suffering, and you know, vaguely, where the pain is coming from. But because the aggression is so well hidden, you are likely to blame yourself instead of the aggressor, and to add to your own misery, like this:

"I can't understand why I feel so *stupid* when I'm with her. She's always so considerate and she's such a nice person! There must be something wrong with me."

In a situation like that there probably is something wrong with you, yes. Your problem is that you are the target of verbal violence and you don't have the least idea how to defend yourself against it. When someone looks you right in the eye and says "You're an idiot!" you know that's verbal abuse and you probably have ways of dealing with it. But when someone smiles at you and says "Even *you* should be able to understand why *that* won't work!" it's not so easy—especially if a few "sweethearts" or "good buddys" or "darlings" are scattered around to confuse you.

We get little or no training in verbal self-defense. Once upon a time anyone who pretended to an education learned it. It was called rhetoric, and if we really went back to the basics, we would have to put it back in our curriculum. (Today a "rhetoric class" usually means a course in writing.) This book is a manual to teach you a verbal martial art. Unlike a number of books now available, it's not intended to train you to attack others or to be violent yourself. Instead, it will teach you how to use your opponent's strength and momentum as tools for your own defense. You will learn to head off verbal confrontations so skillfully that they rarely happen, and you will learn to do so with honor. The person with a black belt in a physical martial art is unlikely to be a violent person. Knowing that you are fully capable not only of defending yourself but also of inflicting harm on others makes you a very careful person—far more careful than you would be if you reacted to every threatening situation with an untrained panic response.

There are four basic principles of verbal self-defense that you need to learn.

FIRST PRINCIPLE: KNOW THAT YOU ARE UNDER ATTACK

You must be able to recognize a situation where you are in danger or actually under attack. If you continually assume that the reason you come out of conversations feeling somehow hurt and depressed is that you are "too sensitive" or "paranoid" or "childish," you won't recognize danger when it's there. If you can always be taken by surprise because you have no idea what verbal aggression is or how to spot it, you are an ideal target. The vast majority of verbal attacks won't even happen if you are trained in verbal self-defense.

Just as the thug who's planning a mugging is likely to back off and change plans after discovering that the victim isn't helpless, so will the verbal mugger look for someone who isn't going to be able or willing to fight back. You need to learn to recognize the signs of verbal violence. You must become so aware of them that you can sense their most subtle indications, often before *any* words are spoken aloud.

SECOND PRINCIPLE: KNOW WHAT KIND OF ATTACK YOU ARE FACING

You must learn to judge and recognize your opponent's weapons, strength, and skill. Obvious characteristics—such as the loudness of someone's voice, an unpleasant facial expression, or the use of openly insulting (or sometimes openly flattering) words—are not reliable indicators of these things. Often a reliance on the "obvious" signs will mislead you completely and leave you defenseless.

THIRD PRINCIPLE: KNOW HOW TO MAKE YOUR DEFENSE FIT THE ATTACK

The response you make has to match your opponent's move. You must choose an appropriate response and an appropriate level of intensity. Not only is there no need for you to waste your energy on a weak opponent with little skill, it's unethical and cowardly for you to do that. You don't go after bunny rabbits with an elephant gun.

And just as it would be foolish to choose a sword as a weapon against someone armed with a machine gun, the verbal weapon should be chosen to fit the situation. The phrase "enough is enough" is not a worn-out platitude in the art of verbal self-defense. On the contrary, there's no excuse for anything more than just exactly enough.

FOURTH PRINCIPLE: KNOW HOW TO FOLLOW THROUGH

You must be able to carry out your response once you've chosen it. For many people, this may be the most difficult part of verbal self-defense, especially when your opponent is, in physical terms, smaller or weaker than you are. We have all been taught to "pick on somebody our own size." In verbal confrontations, it's important to remember that size has little to do with strength and that some of the most skilled of verbal bullies are only six years old.

It will help if you keep firmly in mind that verbal self-defense is a *gentle* art. It's a way of *preventing* violence. When a parent picks up a small child who is just about to whack a playmate over the head with a toy truck, that act is interfering with the child's freedom and is—in a formal and technical sense—the use of force. Especially if, as is often true, the child has to be physically restrained from carrying out his or her plans. Verbal self-defense is like that; except in the most extreme cases, when it's used skillfully it is a *nonviolent* activity and a way of keeping the peace.

It will also help to remember that we now know hostile language is dangerous not only to its target but also to the person dishing it out, and to any innocent bystander who isn't free to leave the scene. You're not doing anyone a kindness when you help them keep the hostile language flying.

If the Fourth Principle is a problem for you, you should be prepared to feel and to work through a certain amount of guilt. You will be attacked; you will use the techniques in this book to defend yourself against your attacker; and then you will feel guilty. Later we will take up some ways of handling this, but for now just accept the fact that it will happen, and that it's a normal reaction.

2

The Five Satir Modes

In order to learn any new skill, you need a set of words—a vocabulary for discussing that skill. In verbal self-defense we're fortunate; much of the vocabulary has already been provided in different contexts, and can now be adapted to our use.

Virginia Satir was one of the foremost therapists in the United States, famous all over the world for her work in family therapy and other types of therapy. In her books she developed a set of terms for common language behavior patterns that she observed repeatedly in people who were trying to communicate when they were tense and anxious and distressed. There are five such patterns in her system; we call them the "Satir Modes." This book is not about therapy, but the terms are just what we need to serve as an essential part of our working vocabulary. They are:

BLAMER MODE

Blamers feel that nobody cares about them, that there is no respect or affection for them, and that people are indifferent to their needs and feelings. Blamers react to this with language behavior patterns intended to demonstrate to others that the Blamers are in charge and the ones with power. They do this because they're convinced that unless they throw their weight around no one will cooperate with them or give them any attention. Typical Blamer speech, either very loud or hissed between clenched teeth, can be:

> *"You never* **consider** *my* **feelings, and I'm** *not* **going to** *put up* **with that!"**

> *"Nobody* **around here** *ever* **pays any attention to** *me! Why is* **that?"**

> *"Why* **do you** *always* **put your**self *ahead* **of everybody else?"**

> *"Why* **don't you ever think about what** *I* **might want? I've had** *all* **of this I'm going to** *take***!"**

> *"Why* **do you always insist on having your** *own way***, no matter** *how* **much it hurts other people? What's the** *matter* **with you?"**

When two Blamers talk to each other, that language interaction is a broad and rapid road to a shouting match or an open exchange of insults and sarcasm, nasty in every way, and the body language that goes with it is just as angry and hostile as the words that are spoken.

PLACATER MODE

Placaters are frightened that other people will get angry with them, go away, and never have anything to do with them again. Placaters don't dare admit this, however. Typical Placater speech is:

> **"Oh,** *you* **know me—***I* **don't care!"**

> **"Whatever anybody else wants to do is** *fine* **with** *me***."**

"**Whatever you say, dear; *I* don't mind.**"

"**Oh, *nothing* bothers *me*! Do whatever you like.**"

"**What do *I* want to do? Oh, *I* don't know . . . . what would *you* like to do?**"

Few conversations are as dead-end and hopeless as two Placaters trying to reach a decision, with a dialogue like this one:

X: "Where should we go for dinner?

Y: "I don't know. Where would *you* like to go?"

X: "Oh, *you* pick! *You* know me, *I* don't care where we go."

Y: "No, really, *you* decide!"

X: "But it doesn't matter to me at *all!*"

Y: "It doesn't matter to me, either, *you* know that."

X: "Seriously, I'd much much rather *you* decided . . ."

[And so on and on . . .]

Whenever you hear anyone referred to as "Good Old So-and-So," there is at least a fifty-fifty chance that Good Old So-and-So is a Placater. As with Blaming, the body language will match the words spoken.

COMPUTER MODE

Computers have one or more emotions that they're not willing to share or are unwilling to admit they're feeling. Often they will try to create the impression that they feel no emotions at all. Except for the troublesome human side of him that made him so interesting, *Star Trek's* Mr. Spock was an excellent example of a Computer. Computers talk like this:

"**There is undoubtedly a simple solution to the problem.**"

"It's obvious that no real difficulty exists here."

"No rational person would be alarmed by this incident."

"Clearly the advantages of this activity have been over-stated."

"Preferences of the kind you describe are rather common in this area."

Computers work hard at never putting "I" in front of an opinion unless they qualify it heavily, as in "I suppose it is at least possible that . . ." And as is true with all the Satir Modes, their body language matches their words; they limit their facial expressions and gestures and body positions. And their intonation (the tune their words are set to) is kept carefully neutral.

DISTRACTER MODE

Distracters are tricky to keep up with, because they don't hold to any of the previous patterns. But they don't require you to learn anything new. What they do is cycle rapidly among the other patterns, shifting from one Satir Mode to another. The underlying feeling of the Distracter is panic:

"I don't know what on earth to say, but I've got to say *something*, and the quicker the better!"

Their surface behavior, verbal and nonverbal, will be a chaotic mix.

LEVELER MODE

Levelers are the most contradictory type of all—either the easiest or the most difficult to handle, depending on the situation. Levelers do just what Dr. Satir's term implies: they *level* with you. What the Leveler says is what the Leveler feels. Sometimes that's safe and appropriate; sometimes it's not.

Suppose we had five terrified people trapped in an elevator that was stuck between floors, one from each of the Satir Modes. Their remarks as the elevator hung there would go something like this:

PLACATER: "Oh, I *hope* I didn't do anything to *cause* this! I sure didn't *mean* to!"

BLAMER: *"Which one* of you idiots was *fooling around* with the *but*tons??"

COMPUTER: "There is undoubtedly some perfectly simple reason why this elevator isn't moving. Certainly there is no cause for alarm."

DISTRACTER: "Did *one* of you hit the *Stop button?* Oh, I didn't *mean* that, of *course* none of you would do anything like that! It is, however, extremely easy to do that sort of thing by accident. *Why* do things like this *always* happen to *me?"*

LEVELER: "Personally, I'm scared."

You will notice one thing about the descriptions of these language behavior patterns. In every one of them except Leveler Mode there's a clash between the inner feelings and the outer behavior. When someone is locked into one of these modes and can't communicate effectively in any other way, he or she may be in emotional difficulty that interferes with clear communication—again, except for the Leveler. Levelers have no trouble communicating their feelings.

Although most people have a Satir Mode they prefer when communicating under stress, they're not restricted to that mode. They can choose, either deliberately or unconsciously, to use any one of the modes at will. When the choice is made deliberately, the classic mismatch between inner feelings and outer behavior may not exist. A person may decide to use Computer Mode because he or she is in a committee meeting and perceives that as an appropriate choice; it doesn't necessarily mean that the person is trying to conceal some emotions. A parent who feels perfectly secure in a position of control over a child may choose Blamer Mode deliberately as a way of disciplining that child. People who are absolutely determined to start a fight know that choosing Blamer or Placater Mode is their best strategy; people whose primary communication goal is to eliminate hostile language from their environment know that it's far better to choose Computer or Leveler Mode.

In this book we won't be concerned with situations where individuals literally aren't *able* to choose which Satir Mode they will use. Those situations are properly left to the expert therapist. We can, however, adapt the category names to the art of verbal self-defense. Like the sword, the gun, the stick, and the hatpin, the Satir Modes are weapons for verbal conflict and mechanisms for heading off such conflict. You need to learn to recognize them when they're coming at you, to choose among them for your response, and to use the ones you choose with confidence and skill.

It's important to remember that a Leveler may not be attacking you and may have no hostile intentions, even when there are surface indicators that might mislead you. For example:

LEVELER: "You know, you drive me crazy tapping your ballpoint pen on the desk like that. It really bothers me."

This is not an attack; it's a simple statement of fact and an invitation for an equally Leveling response. For example:

YOU: "I know what you mean. It would drive me crazy, too. What's even worse is somebody who whistles under their breath all the time."

LEVELER: "You're right. That's even worse. I'd just as soon you didn't do either one."

YOU: "I'll try. Okay?"

LEVELER: "Fair enough."

That's not fighting, it's negotiation. It's very easy to turn it *into* a fight, however. One of the ironies of verbal interaction is that so many people mistake the statements of a Leveler for verbal violence and never suspect that the nice guy or nice lady down the hall is the one who's really giving them a hard time.

It's also important to remember that when we refer to someone with one of the Satir Mode labels, we're only using shorthand. For example, calling someone a "Blamer" isn't like calling that person "a Norwegian" or "a carpenter" or "a bully;" it's just a brief and convenient way to say "someone who—while communicating in a tense or confrontational situation—is using Blamer Mode." The Satir Mode labels aren't labels for personality types.

Keep the Satir Modes in mind as we go along; they are your basic inventory of *stances* for verbal self-defense. Learn to spot them when they're coming at you; learn to choose among them consciously and deliberately as a communication strategy.

In an emergency, when you have no time to think or when you haven't had sufficient training or practice to be sure what your best choice would be, your safest "guess" stance is always Computer Mode, because it is the most neutral of the five modes. *Assume that stance and maintain it until you have a good reason to change.* Here is a summary of the characteristics of Computer Mode. Computers:

- never appear to be angry or emotional or hurried or upset; always look calm and relaxed.

- try never to talk in the first person singular ("I," "me," "my," "mine," "myself") without adding an array of modifying sequences.

- do their best always to talk in abstractions and generalities.
- say, "It's _____ that [X];" for example, "It's obvious that there is no cause for alarm."
- usually take a single physical position early in the conversation and maintain it with little change from then on.
- rarely use emphatic stress on words or parts of words.
- almost never openly commit themselves to anything.

If you don't know what to do when you're under verbal attack, the rule is always: *Switch to Computer Mode and stay there.* There is no safer stance.

ONE MORE TERM

I want to end this chapter by introducing just one more term that we will find useful. When we talk to people, the things we say come in a variety of different shapes and sizes. We may say a whole sentence; we may say only a part of a sentence; we may say only one word. We may say several sentences in a row. We don't feel obligated to follow the rules of written language when we're talking to one another. We therefore need a word that can serve as a name for any sequence of language that takes up a single turn in a conversation or other language interaction. The term I will be using for that purpose in this book is the word "utterance."

"Hello!" is an utterance.

"Oh, blast!" is an utterance.

"I wonder . . ." is an utterance.

"Are you leaving now?" is an utterance.

"If you're leaving now . . ." is an utterance.

"I need a ride home. Are you leaving now?" is an utterance.

And when someone grabs the conversational floor and goes on and on and on without giving anyone else a chance to say anything at all? That too is an utterance.

3

The Verbal Attacks Octagon

One of the major reasons why people don't realize that verbal violence is being used against them is that they've never been taught about presuppositions. They know about them, of course, below their conscious level of awareness. That's why they feel hurt or insulted in response to something that sounds, on the surface, like a nonhostile thing to say. But they've never been taught to watch out for presuppositions, or to pay attention to them instead of just to the words they're hearing. As a result, they can't provide a reasonable explanation of *why* they feel hurt or insulted.

The term "presupposition" is used in a number of different ways by scholars in various fields. So that there will be no confusion, I am going to define it—for this book—as follows:

A presupposition is something that a native speaker of a language knows is part of the meaning of a sequence of that language, even when it is not overtly present in the sequence.

For instance, every native speaker of English knows that the sentence "Even *Bill* could get an A in *that* class" means (a) that Bill is no great shakes as a student, and (b) that the class is not difficult in any way. But notice that *neither one* of those pieces of information is present anywhere in the overt wording of the sentence. That is, the sentence doesn't say, "Even Bill, who is certainly no great shakes as a student, could get an A in that class, which isn't difficult in any way." Nevertheless, that is what the sentence *means*. The two extra pieces are said to be presuppositions of that sentence.

The illustration in Figure 1 is a training device that we will use in this book to make you more aware of presuppositions. Although there are of course other patterns of hostile language, the eight patterns shown on the Verbal Attacks Octagon are some of the most basic and most common. They are eight of the Verbal Attack Patterns of English (which we can call VAPs, rhyming with "maps," for short). Each section of the Octagon shows you a hostile language pattern that has two major parts: at least one open insult that serves as the bait, and one or more chunks of hostile language hidden away as a presupposition of the utterance.

In this chapter we'll go quickly through all eight sections of the Octagon. Then in the chapters that follow, we'll take up each of the patterns in detail and consider strategies for dealing with them.

The most important principle to remember is this one: *Never take the bait.* Ignore the bait and respond to something else, something that is presupposed. The steps of your strategy go like this:

① Notice the Satir Mode that's being used.

② Identify the presuppositions of the utterance.

FIGURE 1: VERBAL ATTACKS OCTAGON

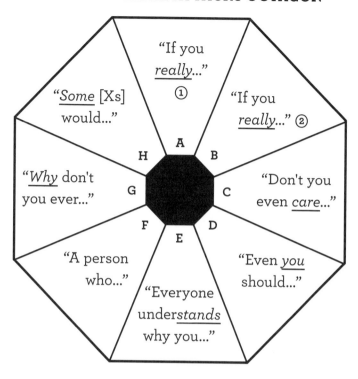

③ Ignore the bait.

④ Respond with a neutral request for information about a pre-supposition or a neutral remark about a presupposition.

⑤ Maintain Computer Mode as much as possible, unless you see that you can safely switch to Leveling.

Now let's go around the Verbal Attacks Octagon briefly, one section at a time, with examples of typical utterances and their relevant presuppositions.

SECTION A

"If you *really* loved me, *you* wouldn't go *bowling* every night!"
PRESUPPOSITION: "You don't really love me."

"If you *really* wanted to lose weight, you wouldn't *eat* so much."

PRESUPPOSITION: "You don't really want to lose weight."

"If you *really* wanted a promotion, you wouldn't *go* to lunch with a person like that!"

PRESUPPOSITION: "You don't really want a promotion."

"If you *really* wanted to pass this course, you'd pay *attention* to my lectures!"

PRESUPPOSITION: "You don't really want to pass this course."

All of these utterances are disguised Blamer Mode sentences. It's a little more subtle to say "If you *really* loved me, you wouldn't go *bowling* every night!" instead of "You don't care anything about me, and the way I know that is that you go bowling every night!" but the meaning is the same. In a Section A attack, the "You don't really . . ." accusation is hidden away as a presupposition.

SECTION B

"If you *really* loved me, you wouldn't *want* to go bowling every night!"

PRESUPPOSITIONS:
- "You don't really love me."
- "You have the power to control not only your actions but also your personal desires."

Section Bs are like an axe dipped in poison. They are Section A attacks escalated to one more level of viciousness, and are of course in Blamer Mode as well.

In the example sentence about going bowling given under Section A, if you stop going bowling every night you've "proved" that you really do love the other person. But "If you *really* loved me, you wouldn't *want* to go bowling every night!" is a verbal trap. Whether you go bowling or not, you are still going to *want* to go. And since you've swallowed the presupposition that if you really loved this person you wouldn't want to go, if you let this attack work you're going to feel guilty no matter what you do. When you go bowling, you'll feel guilty because you're going; when you don't go, you'll feel guilty because you wish you had. Either way, it will take most of the pleasure out of going bowling. The fact that somebody begins this sequence with "Sweetheart" does not turn it into a loving, tender thing to say. When you hear it, you've been attacked. Learn to recognize that.

SECTION C

"Don't you even *care* about your children?"
PRESUPPOSITIONS:
- "You don't care about your children."
- "You *should* care about your children; it's wrong of you not to."
- "Therefore, you should feel rotten."

"Don't you even *care* about your appearance?"

"Don't you even *care* what happens to the other students?"

"Don't you even *care* what the neighbors will tell your mother?"

Section C attacks are straightforward Blamer Mode utterances, even on the surface. It's hard to imagine any of these examples sounding like anything but an accusation.

Notice that the word "care" is heavily stressed in these examples. That's important. It's one way for you to tell the difference between a genuinely interested request for information, such as might come from a Leveler who simply wants to know, and a verbal attack. The presence of our old friend "even" is also a clue.

Take that last example. If it comes from a Leveler, someone who has no hostility in mind, it's likely to take this form:

"Don't you care what the neighbors will tell your mother?"

There's no stress on the word "care," and no "even" in the sentence; the intonation (the melody of the utterance) is very different.

SECTION D

"Even an *elderly* person should be able to understand *this* contract."

PRESUPPOSITIONS:
- "There's some wrong with being an elderly person."
- "It doesn't take much intelligence or ability to understand this contract."
- "You should feel guilty and stupid."

"Even a *woman* should be able to build a *book*shelf."

"Even a *freshman* should be able to pass *this* test."

"Even the *second*-graders know how to do *that*."

And for primitive whacking and slashing:

"Even *you* should be able to follow this argument."

Or:

"Even *you* should be able to follow *this* argument."

You'll have noticed that it's possible to pile up these attacks into multiples. For instance:

"Even a woman who doesn't even *care* about her appearance should be able to understand that stripes only look good on *thin* people!"

This is brutal; if you hear anything like it coming at you, go to Computer Mode and stay there.

The Section D attacks (except when they take the "Even *you* . . ." form) are in mild Computer Mode. Properly done, Section Ds are an abstract reference to a class of individuals, with the same surface shape as a statement like "Even *water* in excess can be poisonous."

SECTION E

"Everyone under*stands* why you're having such a hard time adjusting to this job."

PRESUPPOSITION:

- "Everybody knows about the problem you have that's *causing* your adjustment difficulties, so it's no use trying to hide it or deny it."

"Everyone under*stands* why you're so *emotional* **these days, darling."**

"Everyone under*stands* perfectly why you're getting hysterical, Mrs. Smith."**

This particular type of attack sounds so much like Leveler Mode that it can catch you off guard. The presence of that all-knowing and unidentified "everyone" at the beginning should be a warning; Section E attacks are a mixture of Computer Mode and Blaming.

SECTION F

"A person who really *wanted* **to succeed wouldn't object to a trivial regulation like our** *dress* **code."**

PRESUPPOSITION: "You don't really want to succeed."

"A person who has serious emotional problems can't be *expected* **to cope with the workload here like the** *other* **employees do."**

PRESUPPOSITIONS:

- "You have serious emotional problems."
- "The workload here is reasonable for an individual who doesn't have serious emotional problems."

"A boy who *really* wanted people to know he wasn't a sissy wouldn't sit inside *reading* all the time."

PRESUPPOSITIONS:

- "You don't really care whether people know you're not a sissy."
- "Sissies sit around inside reading all the time."

Section Fs are in Computer Mode form, but their form is misleading; they're really only a skilled variation on Section A attacks. "A person who *really* cared about his job would do it *right*" is less crude than "If you *really* cared about your job, you'd do it *right*." However, the two sentences mean roughly the same thing. In Section Fs, the fact that the attack is aimed at you is presupposed by the intonation and the context. When you are the target of one of these, you'll understand immediately that *you* are the "person who."

SECTION G

"*Why* don't you ever want me to be happy?"

PRESUPPOSITIONS:

- "You don't ever want me to be happy."
- "You have the power to make me happy, when you're willing to use it."
- "Whatever your reason is, I'm telling you in advance that it's not good enough."

Or:

"*Why* do you always want me to be *mis*erable?"

PRESUPPOSITIONS:

- "You always want me to be miserable."
- "You have the power to make me miserable, when you're willing to use it."
- "Whatever your reason is, I'm telling you in advance that it's not good enough."

"*Why* don't you ever think about what *other* people might want?"

"*Why* can't you ever do *anything* right?"

No amount of tinkering will make "*Why* don't you ever..." different enough from "You never..." to remove it from Blamer Mode.

SECTION H

"*Some* husbands would *object* to having their wives go back to school when the kids are just babies."

PRESUPPOSITIONS:

- "It's wrong for you to go back to school."
- "I'm not like other husbands—I'm unique and superior to them because I'm not objecting to your going back to school."
- "You should feel very guilty about going back to school."
- "You should feel very grateful to me for being the way I am."

All this, and Computer Mode as well? That's right. Although the set of presuppositions for a Section H attack is in Blamer Mode, the surface form is Computer Mode. Here are a few more examples of this attack:

"*Some* bosses would *object* to having an employee who always leaves work five minutes early to catch a *bus*."

"*Some* professors would really be *upset* about getting a term paper that wasn't even *typed*."

"*Some* wives would really get *mad* if their husbands went fishing over the weekend and left them home alone."

"*Some* landlords would seriously consider taking *legal* action if they had a tenant who never made any attempt to take care of his apartment."

By no means does this cover all of the possible verbal attack patterns of English. But if you can defend yourself against these eight VAPs, your skills will develop and make it possible for you to respond to attacks you haven't encountered before. When you master the basics and apply them by frequent practice, you're well on your way.

HOW TO USE THE NEXT EIGHT CHAPTERS

Now we are going to move on to take up each Octagon section in detail, one to a chapter. The chapters are carefully designed for your self-training.

Near the beginning of each chapter you will find an octagon like Figure 1, except that its sections have been left blank. As you read the chapter, you will think of examples from your personal life that you want to analyze. If you don't make a note of these, they're likely to slip your mind, and then when you're free to work on them you won't be able to remember what they were. To avoid this, write them down in the sections of the blank octagon as they occur to you.

In each of the Octagon chapters you'll also find a set of journal pages where you can record verbal confrontations from your own life—both what was actually said and what *ought* to have been said. At first you'll be much better at working these out after they're over, when it's too late, than while they're actually going on. This is what makes the journal so valuable. You can try as many different versions of the way the confrontation should have gone as you like, with no additional penalties. You can photocopy these pages to make extra copies if you feel that you need more space.

Finally, each of these chapters contains sample verbal confrontations in which some lines have been left blank for you to fill in. Then, at the end of the chapter, you'll find a set of Sample Scripts—possible ways that the confrontation could have worked out, with an analysis of the verbal moves for each one. After you've filled in the example, you should compare your own solution with the end-of-chapter suggestions, remembering that there will always be many possible "correct" answers.

Let's begin.

4

"If You *Really* . . ." ①

The "If you *really*...." sequence is one of the most elementary verbal attack patterns, and is an excellent place for a novice to start. The pattern for a Section A move looks like this:

"If you *really* [X], you would/wouldn't [Y]."

The *X*s and *Y*s may be filled by almost anything, depending on the situation, but this is the verbal frame into which they will be fit. Any utterance coming at you in this form should immediately alert you to the possibility that you are headed for a verbal confrontation. The stronger the emphatic stress placed on the word "really," the more likely it is that you are under attack. The presupposition that matters is, of course, "You don't really [X]." And what is crucial is that you recognize that presupposition and respond to it, not to the content of [Y]. Whatever fills [Y] is only the *bait*—the element that your opponent is using to distract you and get your attention, and that should be ignored.

Most of the time, the move is successful. That is, the targeted person who doesn't realize that an attack is underway or know

YOUR PERSONAL OCTAGON

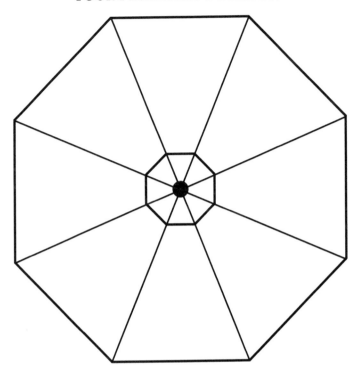

how to handle it takes the bait and responds to [Y]. This is a sure way to lose in the confrontation. Let's look at a very simple and typical example.

CONFRONTATION ONE: *A HUSBAND & WIFE*

TOM: "If you *really* loved me, *you* wouldn't waste so much *money*."

MEG: "I *don't* waste money! Do you have any idea what it *costs* to feed a family these days?"

Meg has already lost this one, no matter what happens from this point on, because she has completely ignored Tom's real challenge—that she doesn't love him. By taking the bait about wasting money instead of responding to that presupposed attack, she has conceded the point and admitted by default that he's right. But let's look at a few more moves all the same, to see what's likely to happen.

TOM: "I notice that your sister manages to feed *her* kids without putting the whole family into bankruptcy!"

MEG: "How would *you* know what my sister spends on food? How would you know what *any*body spends? You never do any grocery shopping, all *you* do is go out to lunch on your expense account and wave your credit cards around and charge it all to your company, and then you come home and complain about what *I* spend!"

TOM: [Very reasonable tone of voice] "Why is it, honey, that whenever we try to have a simple adult discussion of any issue, you always get hysterical and turn it into a fight?"

Meg does speak English, and she did *hear* that presupposition about not loving Tom at the beginning of Confrontation One. Because she heard it and understood it, she knows that she has been attacked and wronged. But because she bungled the interaction and handed him the victory on a platter, it's almost certain that no matter what goes on in the next few moves, the closing lines will include an apology from Meg and a gracious acceptance of that apology from Tom.

Point, set, and match to Tom, you see. Not only doesn't Meg love him, not only has she fallen for his most obvious move, but he has succeeded in tricking *her* into a posture so hostile that she is the one who apologizes. And she has now made a string of open accusations against him that he'll be able to remind her of and use again and again in the future. "Darling," he'll be able to say, "the reason I didn't discuss [X] with you before I did it is because you always get so hysterical. Remember the last time I tried to discuss something with you? I made one little remark about our budget, and in thirty seconds you were *screaming* at me."

If you go through enough episodes like this with your spouse (or parent or employer or teacher or child or employee or friend or anyone else with whom you need to carry on a sustained relationship), a number of unpleasant things will probably happen. You will feel more heavily burdened with guilt with each episode, because you perceive yourself as "always starting fights" with the other person. You feel guilty because you keep hearing yourself—usually to your complete astonishment—making accusations that you know are counterproductive even when they're justified, and making them in a way that leaves you open to the claim that you overreact. You feel guilty because you keep admitting the presupposed attack by default—for example, admitting that you don't love your spouse or don't want to keep your job. The fact that you're not consciously aware of what you're doing doesn't help. The guilt is still there. And piled on top of all this guilt is the guilt you feel because you're convinced that somehow you are the one being abused here, but no matter how you try, you can't put your finger on the source of that conviction. This is an unending vicious and multileveled cycle from which it's very hard to escape.

The relationship between Tom and Meg in the example dialogue may end in separation or divorce. It may end with Meg spending an hour a week with a therapist, or even more hours with a doctor who can never find any explanation for her headaches or her constant indigestion. It may end with Meg becoming bitter and vindictive, famous for her sharp tongue and bad temper, and with Tom getting the sympathy of everyone who knows the two of them intimately.

Tom couldn't get away with a continual campaign of *physical* attacks like this. The bruises and marks he'd leave would be a testimony to his brutality, which would catch up with him in the long run and expose him for the bully that he is. So long as his attacks remain verbal, however, he is not only safe from retribution; he has an excellent chance of being perceived by others as a husband of almost saintly tolerance saddled with a shrewish wife. What's most ironic about this is that he has to do so little to achieve so much. Attacks like the "If you *really* . . ." move are baby tricks and should not have a prayer of success.

I would like to mention two things at this point that it's important to be aware of and to remember. First, Tom may not be consciously aware that he's carrying out this constant verbal battery. He may genuinely believe that he's tolerant and patient and loving, and that Meg is irrational. And we should all be grateful that this is so, because such a man, taught a few elementary facts about language behavior and brought to a conscious realization of his actions, will probably change his ways. He may also be doing it all on purpose, and perhaps enjoying it immensely. There's no way to know which is the case just from looking at one dialogue; we'd need far more information.

Second, Confrontation One has a man as the attacker and a woman as the target. That's not the only possibility. It could easily be the other way around, with the woman attacking and the man as the target. There was a time when men in our culture got a lot of informal training in the use of hostile language and women got almost none. Today that difference has for the most part disappeared. We need only think of Ann Coulter, who is always out there as a potential—and unspeakably dreadful—role model.

If you look at Confrontation One again, you'll see that Tom opens with an attack in mild Blamer Mode. Meg responds immediately to the bait, as he had expected that she would, also in Blamer Mode. Tom comes back with a relatively mild sarcastic

Blamer remark—and Meg escalates into violent Blaming. Tom, now so far out in front that he needn't even exert himself, finishes things off with a Blamer question that is yet one more attack.

Learn this rule early: *Never respond to Blamer Mode with another Blamer Mode utterance.* The only way any Blamer ever beats another Blamer in a verbal fight is by having more sheer force available—being able to yell louder, knowing more rotten and hurtful things to say, being able to keep up an exchange of insults longer without running out of steam, or any similar "advantage." This is exactly like one person beating another in a physical fight because Person A outweighs Person B by sixty pounds and has a bigger club. It's primitive, and it indicates a lack of skill on both sides.

But if Meg should not have replied in Blamer Mode, and should not have taken the bait in the attack, what should she have done instead? One step at a time:

- First principle: *Know that you are under attack.* Hearing the "If you *really* . . ." pattern is signal enough.

- Second principle: *Know what kind of attack you are facing.* Clearly, she wasn't up against much. Any opponent who can't do better for openers than this doesn't have much skill or isn't bothering to try very hard.

- Third principle: *Know how to make the defense fit the attack.* Tom gave her an easy one; she should give him an easy one in return. She should respond to the presupposed attack in a neutral fashion. Look at this revised version of Confrontation One, for clarification.

CONFRONTATION ONE, REVISED

TOM: "If you *really* loved me, *you* wouldn't waste so much *money*."

MEG: "It's interesting that so many men have this feeling that their wives don't love them."

Here Meg has responded in Computer Mode. She hasn't said "I" or "me" or "you"; she hasn't taken the bait and moved to defend the way she spends money. She has shown no emotion beyond a kind of neutral interest, and she hasn't criticized Tom in any way—she's talking about men, and wives, and love, in general.

She has another choice available; she can respond by Leveling.

CONFRONTATION ONE, REVISED AGAIN

TOM: "If you *really* loved me, *you* wouldn't waste so much *money*."

MEG: "When did you start thinking that I don't really love you?"

In this version Meg has again refused to take the bait, but this time she has responded *directly* to the presupposed attack, with a neutral "when" question that does nothing more than repeat what Tom has said to her himself.

When the confrontation goes this way, it may come to a halt almost immediately. For one thing, Meg has the advantage of surprise. Tom won't have expected her to refuse to take the bait. He may change the subject, and the whole argument will have been headed off. The "when" question is an ideal response and is completely nonviolent self-defense.

To be certain that this is clear, let me show you what a violent counterattack would look like.

TOM: "If you *really* loved me, *you* wouldn't waste so much *money*."

MEG: "It's interesting that so many men—once they reach *your* age--begin to feel that their wives don't love them."

This response from Meg is dirty fighting. Anyone who gives in to the temptation to do this kind of thing should be prepared for an immediate escalation of the argument, and should be prepared to handle some serious heavy-duty confrontation. This is a mistake, but many a beginner gets into deep trouble this way because it's so easy and seems so effective at the time. *Resist the temptation.* File the idea away, so that when an utterance like this response is coming at you you'll recognize it for the low blow it is. But don't stoop to using it yourself; you can do much better than that, and with more honor.

About the fourth principle, *Know how to follow through.* If you feel that you can't bring yourself to respond as in the first two revised versions of Confrontation One—perhaps because you can't make yourself ignore the bait about wasting money—things are going to go badly. You really do have to follow through.

One more possible response to the attack in Confrontation One is just to say "Of course I love you." That would be another example of a Leveling response to the first presupposition in the attack. Whenever a Leveling response is true, safe, and appropriate, it's the best choice.

Now let's look at a slightly different example.

CONFRONTATION TWO: *A TEENAGER & HIS FATHER*

LUKE: "If you *really* wanted me to get good grades, *you'd* buy me a com*pu*ter!"

DAD: "A computer! Do you have any idea how much a computer *costs*?"

LUKE: "Jimmy's parents bought *him* a computer. So did Mario's."

DAD: "Jimmy's dad is a *surgeon*. Both of Mario's parents are *lawyers*. They can *afford* to buy computers, or anything else their spoiled kids want!"

LUKE: "So now I'm *spoiled*, and all my friends are spoiled! Just because you couldn't make it through college, just because you're jealous, all of a sudden everybody's a *spoiled kid*! That's really *weird*, you know that?"

DAD: "Whoa! I don't have to take that kind of talk from you!"

LUKE: "That's right, you sure don't! *Remember* that next time you start complaining that I never talk to you about school, *okay*?"

The undisputed winner here is the teenager. By the third move, Dad has completely forgotten that the interaction started out with grades as its topic. Dad has admitted by default the presupposition that he or she doesn't really want Luke to get good grades.

Here's Confrontation Two again, for you to revise. You'll find a set of four possible revisions at the end of this chapter, with comments on each one. After you've written your own dialogue, please compare it with those examples.

CONFRONTATION TWO

LUKE: "If you *really* wanted me to get good grades, *you'd* buy me a computer!"

DAD: _____

_____

LUKE: _____

_____

_____

_____

DAD: _____

_____

_____

_____

LUKE: _____

_____

_____

_____

DAD: _____

_____

_____

_____

You may not need this many moves to finish revising the confrontation, or you may feel that you need more, and that's fine. There are literally an infinite number of possible solutions.

SECTION A ATTACKS ON ME

DATE _____

SITUATION _____

_____

_____

_____

(FIRST MOVE) **WHAT MY OPPONENT SAID**

_____

_____

_____

WHAT I SAID

_____

_____

_____

WHAT I SHOULD HAVE SAID

_____

_____

_____

(SECOND MOVE) **WHAT MY OPPONENT SAID**

_____

_____

_____

WHAT I SAID

_____

_____

_____

WHAT I SHOULD HAVE SAID

_____
_____
_____

(THIRD MOVE) **WHAT MY OPPONENT SAID**

_____
_____
_____

WHAT I SAID

_____
_____
_____

WHAT I SHOULD HAVE SAID

_____
_____
_____

(FOURTH MOVE) **WHAT MY OPPONENT SAID**

_____
_____
_____

WHAT I SAID

_____
_____
_____

WHAT I SHOULD HAVE SAID

_____
_____
_____

CONFRONTATION TWO

LUKE: "If you *really* wanted me to get good grades, *you'd* buy me a com*pu*ter!"

DAD: "Hey . . . when did you start thinking I don't want you to get good grades?"

LUKE: "Well . . . you don't *act* like you care about it. I mean, all the other kids have computers and stuff, and if they get a good grade on a test they get a dollar for it or something. You never do anything like that. You don't even say I did all right, or anything."

DAD: "You know, that's pretty dumb of me. Not the computer part—the reason I don't get you a computer is because we can't afford it right now. But not paying attention to your tests or saying anything about them . . . that's dumb. I'm sorry, and I *do* care about your grades, and from now on I'll do a better job of letting you know that. Fair enough?"

This is well done, and both Luke and his father come out of it ahead. Dad can afford to bend a little bit, but hasn't promised to buy Luke a computer or pay him for his good grades. Luke is now reassured that Dad does care about the grades, even if evidence doesn't turn up in the form of money. It's pretty clear that Luke knows about the money problems and was really only trying to make Dad understand that some attention would be appreciated.

LUKE: "If you *really* wanted me to get good grades, *you'd* buy me a com*pu*ter!"

DAD: "Parents who *really* want their kids to get good grades don't buy them computers. Fooling around on a computer is just a way of getting out of doing your work."

LUKE: "Then how come you use a computer when you bring work home from the office?"

DAD: "That is *not* the same thing at all, and you're not so stupid that you can't tell the difference!"

Dad is the loser here. What he has done is challenge the wrong presupposition—the trivial one that "a parent who wants a kid to get good grades always buys that kid a computer." Dad may feel that the response is a good one, intended to demonstrate that Luke is a reasonable person who can discuss an issue logically. Unfortunately, that's not the way Luke is going to see or hear it. Whatever happens from this point on won't change that, and the most probable outcome is a fight. Dad may "win" in the brute force sense, but it will only be because he is bigger, louder, and has more power. Very poor strategy, and sure to rebound in the long run.

LUKE: "If you *really* wanted me to get good grades, *you'd* buy me a com*pu*ter!"

DAD: "If a computer is what it will take to prove to you that I care about your *grades*, then of *course* I'll buy you one!"

LUKE: "Can I have one like Fred's got? A really good one?"

DAD: "Like I *said*—if that's what it will take, of *course*!"

This variation should be examined carefully. Dad has responded immediately, and directly, to the presupposition in Luke's opening move. But notice how it was done. First, Dad is using Placater Mode in response to a teenager using Blamer Mode, and that's not smart. A Placating response to Blaming is just as counterproductive as another Blaming response. Plus, youngsters don't feel secure when the people they're trying to look up to as role models and sources of stability in their world start Placating at them. Luke is dissatisfied enough to push the Blaming further; his second move is a compressed "If you really *mean* it when you say you care about my grades, you won't just buy me *any* old computer, you'll get me a fancy expensive one!" And Dad makes the same mistake again—more Placating.

And that's not all. If you take a close look at what Dad is saying, you'll notice a new presupposition that's being sneaked in, something like this:

"You're the kind of kid who can only be convinced about my wanting you to get good grades if I *buy* you something, and I don't think much of that."

It's a small dig, going by fast, but it's in there, and Luke will hear it. Especially since Dad goes on to say it again. Nobody won here, and nobody got anything they wanted. It may very well be that what Luke really wants from his father, more than he wants a computer, is reassurance and support; if so, he got neither one. This is a standoff in every way, with the possible exception of the father's finances.

LUKE: "If you *really* wanted me to get good grades, *you'd* buy me a com*pu*ter!"

DAD: "When did you start thinking I don't want you to get good grades? That's a crazy idea!"

LUKE: "I didn't say that! *You* said that! You're always putting words in my mouth that I don't *say*!"

DAD: "Now, getting all excited and starting an argument is not going to help with your grades or anything else. When you're ready to talk like a reasonable person, we'll discuss this again."

Dad's first mistake here was in adding "That's a crazy idea!" to the first response. Up to that point, the response was a neutral request for information. But the "crazy idea" addition is straight Blamer Mode, and it's backed up and reinforced by "When you're ready to talk like a reasonable person . . ." In the sense that Dad doesn't have to buy a computer and has demonstrated superior status in the household, he has won. But the price is a resentful and humiliated teenager who has been able to accuse Dad of caring nothing about his grades and gotten away with it, and has also been treated with total disrespect. This is a recipe for parent/child communication breakdown.

5

SECTION B ATTACKS:

"If You *Really* . . ." ②

Going from Section A attacks to Section B attacks won't be difficult, because Section Bs are only Section As with the power turned up one notch. Your practice with the examples in Chapter Four—in your journal pages and in your daily life—will let you move through this chapter with ease and confidence. Keep the Four Principles in mind; keep the Satir Modes in mind; and practice. The pattern for a Section B move looks like this:

"If you *really* **[X], you** *would/wouldn't want* **to [Y]."**

Or, to make it just a tad meaner:

"If you *really* **[X], you wouldn't even** *want* **to [Y]."**

Or: **"If you** *really* **[X], you would at** *least want* **to [Y]."**

There are two presuppositions in the basic sequence that you need to pay attention to. The first one is already familiar: "You don't really [X] . . ." And then there is this additional one:

"You have the power to control not only your actions but also your personal desires."

YOUR PERSONAL OCTAGON

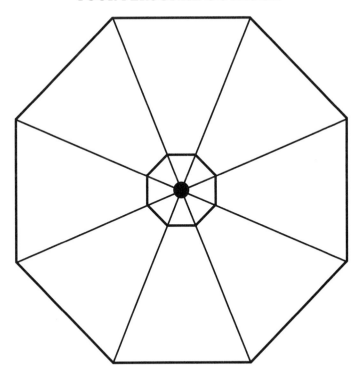

The first presupposition may or may not be true, depending on whether you really do or do not love someone, want to get good grades, want to be promoted, want to make the football team, or whatever is the content of [X]. The second presupposition, however, is *always false.*

All of us are able to exercise our willpower to a certain extent. We may be quite capable of turning down that second piece of cake. We may be equally able to stay out of that poker game we were invited to join. We may be able to give up our favorite video game. But none of us, because we are human and because desire is part of being human, is able to deliberately *not want* the piece of cake or *not want* to join our friends in the poker game or *not want* to play the video game. We may be able to distract ourselves by eating four carrots instead of the cake or by going fishing instead of turning to the poker game or video game, thus making the desire a little less intense—but the wanting won't go away. That's the nature of being human, and if you're free of that trait you certainly don't need to read this book.

In a Section B confrontation you'll have no trouble recognizing that you're under attack. There's "If you *really* . . ." to let you know something's up, and once you've spotted the two presuppositions you know what you're dealing with. The level of skill and strength shown is slightly higher than a Section A move, but it's nothing formidable. You know that the proper way to handle it is to respond to a presupposition, preferably with no hostile language at all. But *which* presupposition? The Section B move offers you two to choose from.

The answer is that it depends. Which one is the stronger attack on you? Which one bothers you most? Which one seems the easier to take on? You have ample time to move against both if you like, and it makes no particular difference which one you start with. This is nothing to be concerned about; choose one, and then go on to the other if it turns out to be necessary.

Here's an example for you:

CONFRONTATION THREE: *A MOTHER & DAUGHTER*

MOM: "If you *really* cared about my health, *you* wouldn't *want* to dress the way you do!"

JANICE: "There is nothing wrong with the way I dress except that *you're* too old to understand what a young woman *ought* to wear!"

MOM: "*What?* I am *not* old, and if I wasn't so sick I wouldn't *look* old! How can you *be* so cruel?? My own daughter!

But never mind—*you* know me, I don't care about *any-thing any more!*"

JANICE: Mom, I didn't mean that you look old; I didn't mean *any* of that the way it sounded. Oh, Mom, don't cry, *please* don't cry! You know how I am, I say things before I think; I never did have any sense. You *know* I wouldn't hurt you, not for anything in the world!"

MOM: "No, no, it's *my* fault, and you're right: I'm an old woman, and I'm holding you back. But I won't be here much longer, and then you'll be able to wear whatever you want to wear, without having to listen to me complaining about it."

JANICE: "Oh, heavens! Mom, you *know* I don't care what I wear! Come on, now—what do you hate the most? You tell me, and I'll throw it away. *Please*?"

Notice the sequence of moves here:

- Mom opens in Blamer Mode.
- Janice falls for it, takes the bait, and responds by counter-attacking in Blamer Mode herself. She ignores the presuppositions and concedes both that she doesn't care about her mother's health and that she's able to control her desires—which is admitting by default that she deliberately mistreats her mother.
- Mom grabs her opportunity and surges into Distracter Mode, raining blows in all directions.
- Janice panics, and demonstrates that panic by switching to Placating.
- Mom does a touch of phony Placating and then twists the

knife in for a final Blamer attack: Janice, she claims, is just hanging around waiting for her mother to die so that Janice can dress like a fool and spend the rest of her life doing that.

- Janice, now completely demoralized, goes into the most extreme Placater style she can muster, and ends by begging for a chance to prove that she isn't really a monster.

The mother in this example is guilty of blatant child abuse, although her attacks leave no visible bruises. If she's good at what she does, she may manage to live out her life viewed by one and all as a devoted parent mistreated and neglected by her ungrateful selfish child. Because she's a woman, she will eventually have the cultural stereotype of the Constantly Complaining Elderly Woman to deal with. But if she does it with dignity and elegance (yes, this is possible), and if daughter Janice makes one stupid communication mistake after another, her chances of success are very good.

Now, let's consider what Janice might have done instead.

CONFRONTATION THREE, REVISED

MOM: "If you *really* cared about my health, *you* wouldn't *want* to dress the way you do!"

JANICE: "The idea that people don't care about other people's health is interesting, don't you think? It would seem that any human being would just naturally be concerned about the well-being of other people . . . but just look at the state of health care in this country!"

Here Janice has responded in Computer Mode directly to the first presupposition. Mother and daughter are now in the midst of a philosophical discussion of an abstract question, instead of a personal confrontation. Another possible Computer Mode move, but responding to the second presupposition, would go like this:

MOM: "If you *really* cared about my health, *you* wouldn't *want* to dress the way you do!"

JANICE: "You know, the idea that people are able to control not only their actions but also their personal desires is really interesting."

Alternatively, Janice might prefer to make her first move a response in Leveler Mode, with a neutral "when" question and neutral body language, like this:

JANICE: "Mom, when did you start thinking that I don't care about your health?"

Or:

JANICE: "Mom, have you always thought that people can control both their actions *and* their personal desires?"

The Leveler stance is useful here, but it has to be done with care. Any mistake in tone of voice or facial expression, and the utterance will sound like Blaming instead of Leveling. Above all, be sure you don't throw any "evens" into one of these, as in this example:

JANICE: "Mom, when did you first decide that I don't even care about your health?"

Other question words are also available for use in this move. For instance:

"Where did you get the idea that I don't care about your health?"

"Why do you suppose you feel that I don't care about your health?"

"What makes you think I don't care about your health?"

But I advise against these; each one (and the rest of the set) carries with it a presupposition. "Where did you get the idea . . ." presupposes "You got the idea that I don't care about your health *some*where, and I want to know where that was." "Why do you suppose you feel . . ." and "What makes you think . . ." presuppose "You have some reason for feeling that I don't care about your health, and I want to know what it is."

A "when" question also has a presupposition—"There was some time when you started thinking I don't care anything about your health"—but it only repeats what your opponent has just said to you and it's not as likely to lead you somewhere you don't want to go. A "when" question usually leaves your opponent only two choices: Either answer the question as if it were a neutral request for information, or deny its presupposition. Like this:

JANICE: "Mom, when did you start thinking that I don't care about your health?"

MOM: "When you were thirteen years old, *that's* when! Don't you remember the time that . . .?"

And with any luck at all, Mom will head off into an anecdote and Janice will be able to follow her and shift to another subject entirely.

JANICE: "Mom, when did you start thinking that I don't care about your health?"

MOM: "I never *said* I thought you didn't care about my health! I was *talking* about the disgusting way you *dress*!"

Now Mom will probably move into a lengthy lecture on proper clothing; but whatever happens, she has given up her presupposed attack claiming that Janice is indifferent to her state of health. And Janice has the option of heading off the clothing lecture with a phony stance, like this:

JANICE: "Mom, when did you start thinking that I don't care about your health?"

MOM: "I never *said* I thought you didn't care about my health! I was *talking* about the disgusting way you *dress!*"

JANICE: "Isn't it amazing how often I misunder*stand* you, dear? I'll really try from now on to pay better attention to what you're saying."

Janice has done very well, although it may at first glance look to you as if she has surrendered. She hasn't admitted either that she can control her personal desires or that she cares nothing about her mother's state of health. She has led the confrontation away from both her mother's health and her own style of dress, and she hasn't agreed to change that style of dress in any way whatsoever. Finally, she has demonstrated what a good daughter she is by admitting the minor flaw of failing to pay close enough attention when spoken to, and promising to try to do better in the future. Her mother may not be taken in by any of this, but for her to work her way back to either of the two attacks she started with would require her to behave like a shrew in response to the Good Daughter demonstration, and that is not the way to win.

A vicious counterattack in response to the opening line in Confrontation Three would go like this:

JANICE: "When a woman reaches *your* age, dear, she often starts thinking that nobody cares anything about her health and well-being. It's *very* common and understandable, and you mustn't worry about it for a single minute."

This is never justified. Never. As in any other martial art, un-necessary force is dishonorable and merely indicates that you are either an amateur or a sadist. Even as an effort to protect someone else who is clearly at the mercy of a vindictive parent, and is attacking her own child right in front of you, it's not justified. Furthermore, if you try to help in a situation like that, don't be surprised if the daughter turns on you and defends her attacker. That's a pretty standard script, especially if the targeted person is unaware that she's a target and the attacks have been going on for years. If that happens, *let it pass.* You can afford to be generous, and she probably cannot.

Finally, there is one more Leveler option: a direct, firm, and neutral response to the first presupposition. Like this:

MOM: "If you *really* cared about my health, *you* wouldn't *want* to dress the way you do!"

JANICE: "Of course I care about your health."

If that's true—if you do in fact care about what you've been accused of being indifferent to—that's an excellent move.

Now, here's a sample confrontation for you to work on, followed by some suggested scripts.

CONFRONTATION FOUR: *A SUPERVISOR & HER EMPLOYEE*

MISS STEIN: "If you *really* cared about being promoted, you'd *want* to get your reports in on time, like everybody *else* in the department."

KIM: _____

_____

_____

_____

MISS STEIN: _____

_____

KIM: _____
_____
_____
_____
_____
_____

MISS STEIN: _____
_____
_____
_____

KIM: _____
_____
_____
_____

SECTION B ATTACKS ON ME

DATE _____

SITUATION _____

_____

_____

_____

(FIRST MOVE) WHAT MY OPPONENT SAID

_____

_____

_____

WHAT I SAID

_____

_____

_____

WHAT I SHOULD HAVE SAID

_____

_____

_____

(SECOND MOVE) WHAT MY OPPONENT SAID

_____

_____

_____

WHAT I SAID

_____

_____

_____

WHAT I SHOULD HAVE SAID

_____
_____
_____

(THIRD MOVE) **WHAT MY OPPONENT SAID**

_____
_____
_____

WHAT I SAID

_____
_____
_____

WHAT I SHOULD HAVE SAID

_____
_____
_____

(FOURTH MOVE) **WHAT MY OPPONENT SAID**

_____
_____
_____

WHAT I SAID

_____
_____
_____

WHAT I SHOULD HAVE SAID

_____
_____
_____

CONFRONTATION FOUR

MISS STEIN: "If you *really* cared about being promoted, you'd *want* to get your reports in on time, like everybody *else* in the department."

KIM: "Miss Stein, have you always felt that I had no interest in being promoted?"

MISS STEIN: "No . . . Frankly, my first reaction to you was that you were someone with a lot of ambition. I expected you to get ahead in the department and to do that pretty quickly."

KIM: "I wonder what caused you to question your original judgment, Miss Stein. Ordinarily you trust your perceptions of your staff, and that policy seems to have had only positive results for the firm."

Kim has done this well. Her supervisor is now in a tight position for her next move. She may of course move right in with a response like this:

MISS STEIN: "Thank you; I appreciate the compliment. However, in *your* case I was clearly mistaken."

If that happens, however, Kim has nevertheless managed one important and positive result—Miss Stein has switched to Leveler Mode, and it should now be possible to discuss the issue more openly and reasonably. Kim has not made the mistake of taking the bait and arguing about either the timing of her own reports or whether it's true that everybody else's reports are always on time; instead, she has responded to the first presupposition. Furthermore, although she has complimented Miss Stein, it wasn't an excessive Placating gush. Miss Stein may be willing to accept it and unwilling to present the idea that she's been mistaken in her perceptions this time. In either case, Kim is now in a better position to discuss whatever is the real reason behind Miss Stein's attack.

MISS STEIN: "If you *really* cared about being promoted, you'd *want* to get your reports in on time, like everybody *else* in the department."

KIM: "Miss Stein, where did you get the idea that I'm not interested in a promotion?"

MISS STEIN: [Icily] "If you are suggesting that I have listened to gossip about you, or anything of that nature, I suggest you think carefully before you say anything more. I *despise* office gossip."

KIM: "Oh, I didn't mean to suggest *any*thing like *that*, Miss Stein!"

To which, I'm afraid, the most likely response is "Then why *did* you suggest it?"

Kim has properly moved to respond to the presupposition in this confrontation. However, what happened is typical of the hazards of asking any question other than a "when" question. Since the person using a Section B attack has already agreed to the claim being made after "If you *really* . . .", that agreement has to have had a starting point in time. Asking about that point is therefore not a challenge. This strategy may be boring, but your goal in a workplace situation where you're outranked should not be excitement. Your goal is to avoid hostile language as far as possible, to do so honorably, and when it cannot be avoided, to handle it in such a way that you cease to be its target without yourself becoming an attacker. Stay with the "when" questions; they are the most neutral choice.

MISS STEIN: "If you *really* cared about being promoted, you'd *want* to get your reports in on time, like everybody *else* in the department."

KIM: "Miss Stein, do you really believe that people have the ability to control their desires as well as their actions?"

MISS STEIN: "I beg your pardon?"

KIM: "I mean, when did you start thinking that people have control over what they *want* to do?"

Kim has slipped badly here and has chosen the wrong presupposition to ask questions about. Miss Stein is understandably bewildered by the whole exchange, and things are only going to go downhill from here. You would only take up the question of whether people can control their desires when the issue being discussed is food or drink or sex or gambling or some behavior of equal importance. The idea of anyone agonizing over whether they do or do not want to get their reports in on time, or resisting the temptation to get them in late or early, is preposterous. Kim can only come out of this looking ridiculous.

MISS STEIN: "If you *really* cared about being promoted, you'd *want* to get your reports in on time, like everybody *else* in the department."

KIM: "Miss Stein, when did you begin to feel that I am not interested in a promotion?"

MISS STEIN: "I should think that would be obvious—when you began turning your reports in late."

KIM: "Perhaps a specific incident would be helpful, Miss Stein."

You can always hope that this won't happen. Whether it happens or not has much to do with whether Miss Stein is justified in complaining about the lateness of your reports or not, as well as whether that lateness is unique to you and not shared by your colleagues. However, if you aren't going to be able to avoid dealing with the accusation, you're far better off discussing a specific occasion when it's claimed that you were at fault. You may be able to explain that instance to your supervisor's satisfaction and convince her that it's not part of a pattern but an isolated event. On the other hand, if it *is* part of a general pattern, and you have no excuse, the fact that you're able to discuss it reasonably may win you some time to improve your performance. If Miss Stein can't come up with a specific incident and is forced to admit that, you have gained a point or two. It's too early in this one to know who will win, but given Kim's second move, things are progressing as they should. You should stay in Computer Mode unless it becomes possible to move to genuine Leveling, and you should try to carry this off with as much dignity as the facts of the matter will allow.

One word of warning: The most counterproductive move you could make would be to go for the last succulent morsel of the bait and maneuver yourself into an argument about whether other employees get their reports in on time. Don't make that mistake. Even if you know for a fact that half the staff is always later with reports than you are, saying so will only make things worse. Let the bait pass, even if your supervisor makes an all-out effort to force you to take it. If you find yourself obliged to say, "Miss Stein, I don't talk about other people behind their backs," you may feel that you're risking insolence and asking for trouble.

On the contrary—you will be respected for it. Failing to take that position will earn you nothing but a negative reaction, whether it shows in the surface responses made to you or not.

6

SECTION C ATTACKS:

"Don't You Even *Care* . . ."

This attack is a bit more sophisticated than the Section A and Section B attacks. Its basic form is like this:

"Don't you even *care* about [X]?"

Or: *"Don't* **you even** *care* **about [X]?"**

Possible fillers for [X] are infinite in number. Here are some typical examples:

"Don't you even *care* about your *grades*?"

"Don't you even *care* about your *children*?"

"Don't you even *care* about your *patients*?"

"Don't you even *care* about your responsi*bility* to your *colleagues*?"

"Don't you even *care* about global *warming*?"

In skilled hands, the range of [X] is awe-inspiring, with items such as "Don't you even *care* about the *count*less generations still to *come* who will have to pay the *price* for your misguided *actions*?" representing a middle level of intensity.

YOUR PERSONAL OCTAGON

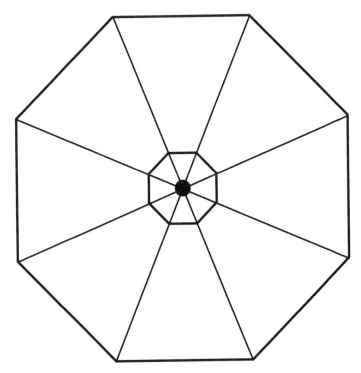

The PRESUPPOSITIONS that go with Section C moves are these:

- **"You don't care about [X]."**

- **"You *should* care about [X]; it's rotten of you not to."**

- **"Therefore, you should feel very guilty and ashamed."**

As you would suspect, the presence of the word "even" hammers in the third presupposition.

Section C sequences that don't include "even" are considerably less hostile. Coming from a Leveler they may be not be VAPs at all; they may be nothing more than a rude and awkward—but neutral—request for information about your feelings. When you hear a Section C with "even" in it, however, and with the heavy emphatic stress on "care," you can be confident that the question isn't neutral.

You'll notice a specific difference between this move and the Section B move. Both have more than one presupposition for you to deal with. But in "If you *really* [X], you would/wouldn't *want* to [Y]" there doesn't have to be any relationship between [X] and [Y]. They are independent of each other, and almost anything the targeted person is vulnerable to can be used to fill the [Y] slot. This isn't true with a Section C move; here the second and third presuppositions are linked with the first. Obviously, if your opponent is wrong and you *do* care about [X], then the second and third presuppositions are irrelevant.

There are a number of possible ways to handle a Section C attack. A crude but effective move, if you don't mind following through on it, is this one:

CHAIR: "Don't you *even* care about the *other members of this committee?*"

MEMBER: "No; why?"

There are times when a less-than-subtle move can be useful. The biggest advantage of this response is its shock value. Look again at the presuppositions of a Section C, and the reason that "No; why?" can be an effective response will be clear. The person coming at you with a Section C is relying on you to go along with the idea that nobody with even a shred of human decency could possibly disagree with those presuppositions. Nobody. Your opponent expects you to agree that the item in [X] is something everyone agrees with, that not to go along with that is wicked, and that anyone guilty of refusing to go along with it should feel like a worm and beg to be stepped on. Your anticipated response is a furious claim that *of course* you care about [X], and how *dare* your opponent suggest that you don't—which is taking the bait and giving your attacker the confrontation that was his or her goal in the first place. Unless you have a reputation as a sociopath or an eccentric, the possibility that you won't go along with this script will never have entered your opponent's head. Your opponent will be startled, and that can be useful. For instance:

CONFRONTATION FIVE: *A TEACHER & A STUDENT'S FATHER*

MS. NORTON: "Don't you even *care* about your little girl *flunk*ing *out* of third *grade*?"

FRANK LEWIS: "No; why?"

MS. NORTON: [Stunned silence] "But you can't possibly *mean* that! You're a good parent, and you *love* your daughter!"

MR. LEWIS: [Maintains neutral expression of polite interest, but says nothing at all]

MS. NORTON: "Look, let me explain to you what it means for a child to flunk a grade and get kept back. *First* of all . . ."

This parent is ahead. Ms. Norton has lost track of the fact that the opening line was an attack on his moral fitness. What Ms. Norton will do now is present a lecture on the problems a flunking child faces—any flunking child at all, not just the one associated with Mr. Lewis. The confrontation has been successfully toned down from a personal attack to a philosophical discussion. Mr. Lewis, if skillful, will agree with everything Ms. Norton says that is remotely sensible, and at the first opportunity will increase the degree of distance between the personal and the philosophical. For example:

MR. LEWIS: "You know, you're absolutely right, and it takes someone with your training and experience to re-alize the implications of these matters. And as long as you've brought it up, don't you think that everything you're saying also applies to college students? Sure, they're adults, but even so, it seems to me that—"

MS. NORTON: "Certainly! Many people don't realize the burden that an F in just one course places on a hard-working student. When I took Logic, for exam-ple—now please remember that I was a straight-A student in every other class I had in college—but when I took *Logic* . . ."

Only after Mr. Lewis is long gone will Ms. Norton realize that no person who was unconcerned about the possibility of his child's flunking third grade would have spent half an hour dis-cussing in depth the dreadful consequences of flunking.

What happens next in the ongoing relationship between parent and teacher (not to mention the one between parent and flunking child) depends on the real-world situation. But the move itself should be clear to you. However, it has one flaw that has to be pointed out immediately: you can never use it twice with the same opponent. If you try it a second time, you're going to hear any icy "You *surely* don't think you can put that over on me *again,* do you?" Precisely because it's such a surprise the first time, and precisely because it is so crude, it will be remembered. Its effectiveness is probably limited even in the sense that you can only use it with one member of a given group. Otherwise, you're likely to hear this: "You surely don't think you can get past *me* with that just because you managed to put it over on Ms. *Nor*ton, do you?" But it has its place, and when you are in that place, by all means use it.

A possibility with a wider application is to respond immediately to the first presupposition, but not by denying it. Instead, respond with a "when" question, or a more elaborate question. As in this dialogue between an employee and his boss:

JOSE LOPEZ: "Don't you even *care* about the way *sales* have been dropping off in your de*partment*?"

ANDY DRAKE: "Pardon me, Mr. Lopez—when did you first start thinking that I had no interest in our sales figures?"

Or:

ANDY: "Do you see this indifference to the sales figures as a general problem, Mr. Lopez, or do you feel that it's confined to the division chiefs in the PQR plant?"

Or:

ANDY: "That question is certainly worth exploring, sir; however, before any attempt can be made to answer it there's the problem of actually putting one's finger on the *cause* of this indifference to sales figures that you've noticed. A number of factors that might account for it come to mind, but your perception of the matter—the way it looks from where you sit—would be a valuable source of preliminary data."

If we gave belts in verbal self-defense, each of the three replies above would represent a more highly-valued belt color. And the strategy could certainly be carried much farther. In business or professional contexts, one of your surest responses to a Section C is a question *about* the first presupposition (that you "don't even *care*"), as heavily larded with the jargon of your field as you can make it. If you can do this entirely in Computer Mode, with no hint of personal involvement or emotion anywhere, you have an excellent chance of leaving your opponent exhausted in three moves.

When a totally abstract Section C move comes at you, in business or in any other language environment, your response should take advantage of that abstractness. For example:

ATTACKER: "Don't you even *care* about the *thousands* of people who go to bed *hungry* in this country *every night?*"

This is a *low* thing to say. Of course you care. The idea that you don't, that perhaps you sit at night stuffing your face with chocolates and chuckling over the image of tiny children crying with swollen bellies in the slums of the world, giggling over the elderly couple splitting a can of cat food for dinner—that's repulsive. For somebody to accuse you of that is inexcusable. The very last thing you should do is stoop to quibbling over how much you care. A little or a lot; 3.2 on a scale from 1 to 5. Don't fall for this. Instead, say:

"Which study are you thinking of, Pat? The Calumet Institute Report or the one from the Borogrovian Center for Social Research?"

And feel free to make up the names of both studies if you don't have real ones on the tip of your tongue. People who do this sort of thing have surrendered their right to meticulous honesty on your part. Stoutly maintain, in the face of all queries, that you are *shocked* to hear that your opponent hasn't even read the studies (the "even" is important). After all, a person who really *cared* about hunger in the world would at least keep up with the literature on the subject, right?

Now, here are two practice dialogues for you to work on, followed by sample scripts.

DR. FREEMAN: "Don't you even *care* about the effect your *smoking* has on the *health* of your *husband* and *children*?"

LYNN WHEELER: _____
_____
_____
_____

DR. FREEMAN: _____
_____
_____
_____

MS. WHEELER: _____
_____
_____
_____

DR. FREEMAN: _____
_____
_____
_____

MS. WHEELER: _____
_____
_____
_____

CONFRONTATION SEVEN:

A MOTHER & HER COLLEGE STUDENT SON

MOTHER: "Don't you even *care* what your father will say when he hears that you're dropping out of school? Don't you even *care* how that's going to make him *feel*?"

PHIL: _____

_____

_____

_____

MOTHER: _____

_____

_____

_____

PHIL: _____

_____

_____

_____

MOTHER: _____

_____

_____

_____

PHIL: _____

_____

_____

_____

SECTION C ATTACKS ON ME

DATE _____

SITUATION _____

_____

_____

_____

(FIRST MOVE) WHAT MY OPPONENT SAID

_____

_____

_____

WHAT I SAID

_____

_____

_____

WHAT I SHOULD HAVE SAID

_____

_____

_____

(SECOND MOVE) WHAT MY OPPONENT SAID

_____

_____

_____

WHAT I SAID

_____

_____

_____

WHAT I SHOULD HAVE SAID

_____

_____

_____

(THIRD MOVE) WHAT MY OPPONENT SAID

_____

_____

_____

WHAT I SAID

_____

_____

_____

WHAT I SHOULD HAVE SAID

_____

_____

_____

(FOURTH MOVE) WHAT MY OPPONENT SAID

_____

_____

_____

WHAT I SAID

_____

_____

_____

WHAT I SHOULD HAVE SAID

_____

_____

_____

CONFRONTATION SIX

DR. FREEMAN: "Don't you even *care* about the effect your *smoking* has on the *health* of your *husband* and *children*?"

LYNN WHEELER: "Well, *he* smokes *too*. Why don't you talk to *him* about smoking?"

DR. FREEMAN: "Because he isn't my patient. *You* are my patient."

MS. WHEELER: "Well, it's not fair."

The patient here has swallowed the bait, admitted by default that she doesn't care what her smoking does to her family members' health (which is very unlikely to be true), and has done her best to dump part of the blame on one of the people she's accused of endangering. There *are* worse ways of handling this, but not many.

DR. FREEMAN: "Don't you even *care* about the effect your *smoking* has on the *health* of your *husband* and *children*?"

MS. WHEELER: "Yes, I do—of *course* I do. You know perfectly *well* that I care about that! And I very much resent your attempt to make me feel even worse about it than I do already."

DR. FREEMAN: "Then why in the world do you go on *smok*ing?"

MS. WHEELER: "Because, as you are also perfectly well aware, I am addicted to cigarettes."

Lynn Wheeler is winning, but not by the usual techniques. The verbal confrontation between doctor and patient in the Western world, especially when the doctor and patient are not the same biological gender, is one of the two or three trickiest interactions in the world of communication. This patient ought to be safe Leveling with the doctor—that's why she goes to him, presumably, to tell him the truth and pay him for using his expertise to help her with whatever problems that truth may involve. Ms. Wheeler has tackled this situation head on and informed Dr. Freeman that she won't tolerate his attempt to increase the guilt she already feels by asking her questions to which he already knows the answers. She is announcing, "I won't play that game." And she is fully justified in taking that position. However, there probably exists no situation between any doctor and patient in which the doctor doesn't have most of the power. As a result, the usual rules don't hold, and patients need to be exceedingly careful.

DR. FREEMAN: "Don't you even *care* about the effect your *smoking* has on the *health* of your *husband* and *children*?"

MS. WHEELER: "No. Why?"

DR. FREEMAN: "Hmmmmmmmmm. [Makes a note in her chart.]

MS. WHEELER: "Well?"

Lynn Wheeler is not only losing, but is in serious trouble. A doctor, because of his or her unique status in our society, is the wrong person to try this on. Nor is any doctor someone on whom to try dropping the names of research studies—real *or* phony—on the dangers of secondhand smoking. The doctor will have read the important studies, and will know the facts. The patient is going to end up in very deep water with such maneuvers. There'll be a note in her chart that says "Patient states that she is indifferent to the harm her smoking may cause to her family's health." And it will be followed by what Dr. Freeman thinks that indicates about the *patient's* physical and/or emotional health. The patient has goofed.

DR. FREEMAN: "Don't you even *care* about the effect your *smoking* has on the *health* of your *husband* and *children*?"

MS. WHEELER: "You've been my doctor for six years now, if my memory serves me right. When did you start thinking that I was indifferent to my family's health?"

DR. FREEMAN: "After the fiftieth time I told you you had to quit smoking, explained to you that you were endangering not only your own health but that of everyone in your family, and saw you go right on smoking."

MS. WHEELER: "A doctor ought to know better than that. Does your experience and research lead you to believe that it's possible to cure addictions by the use of logical arguments? If that's true, the news hasn't yet trickled down to the general public."

This is well done, and Lynn Wheeler is—probably—winning. There is, however, the outside possibility that Dr. Freeman will be so angry at her attempt to even up the dominance relations between them that he will make a little note like this one in the chart: "Patient appears belligerent when challenged on her refusal to comply with medical orders to stop smoking." Dr. Freeman's reaction will almost certainly depend not on the words Lynn spoke in that last response but on *how* those words were spoken. They need to be spoken neutrally, in Leveler Mode, with no hint of sarcasm or any other negative emotion.

MOTHER: "Don't you even *care* what your father will say when he hears that you're dropping out of school? Don't you even *care* how that's going to make him *feel*?"

PHIL: "No. Do you think I should care?"

MOTHER: "What kind of monster *are* you, *any*way? As hard as your father has worked to pay for your education, the things he's done without—how can you sit there and face me and say that you don't *care*?"

PHIL: "Because, Mother, it happens to be the truth. I'm not all that proud of it, but it's the truth. It was Dad's idea for me to go to college, not mine, and it was a rotten idea from the very beginning. The sooner we put it out of its misery, the better off everybody—including Dad—will be."

This is properly done, although Phil may feel miserable doing it. Mother here is doing a classic Blaming attack and, if allowed to continue, will soon bring in Dad's heart condition and the time he walked five miles through a blizzard to buy Phil something or other for Christmas, and so on, far into the night. It has to be made clear to her, as gently as possible, that this won't work. If Phil is telling the truth and the whole college scheme was Dad's idea and is never going to go anywhere but downhill, then it should be brought to an end. It may make Dad feel awful, but not as awful as he will feel if it goes on. College isn't what everyone wants or needs, nor should it be; and if it's all wrong for this student, no favors are being done for anyone by continuing to throw good money (and energy) after bad. Phil is Leveling, and is handling this attack properly.

MOTHER: "Don't you even *care* what your father will say when he hears that you're dropping out of school? Don't you even *care* how that's going to make him *feel*?"

PHIL: "When did you start thinking I don't care anything about Dad's feelings, Mother?"

MOTHER: "When you stopped even pre*tend*ing to do your schoolwork and started spending all your time fooling around at parties and acting the way you do!"

PHIL: "Then why don't we talk about that? It seems to me that that's what's bothering you most."

It's hard to know exactly where this interaction will go—at the moment, it's a standoff. Phil has, quite properly, questioned the presupposed hostile sequence instead of taking the bait. Mother has responded with even more Blaming and has accused him of several unpleasant things. Phil has worded the second response carefully and neutrally, which is a wise strategy. Saying anything like "Then let's talk about *that*, since it's *obviously* what's *really* bothering you!" would only provoke more anger and lead to a brawl instead of the reasonable discussion that's needed.

MOTHER: "Don't you even *care* what your father will say when he hears that you're dropping out of school? Don't you even *care* how that's going to make him *feel*?"

PHIL: "That's an idea you hear a lot: that somebody who drops out of school after their parents make a lot of sacrifices just for that purpose isn't even *bothered* about it. But I never expected to hear it from *you*, Mother."

MOTHER: "Oh? Why not?"

PHIL: "Because you're not the kind of person who would

make that kind of stereotyped judgment."

Well done. Mother has been courteously complimented, the presupposed "you don't care anything about your father" has been challenged, and all is going as it should. The next move is up to Mother, who is going to have to change strategies.

MOTHER: "Don't you even *care* what your father will say when he hears that you're dropping out of school? Don't you even *care* how that's going to make him *feel*?"

PHIL: "Now you're going to start laying all those guilt trips on me, *aren't* you?"

MOTHER: "I beg your pardon?"

PHIL: "First you're going to tell me how hard you and Dad worked to get me into college. Then you're going to tell me that you never took a vacation, not even once, so there'd be enough money for my tuition. Right? Then you're going to start on Dad's heart condition, and how that's all my fault, and *then*, Mother darling, you're going to finish it off by telling me that if I drop out of school it will kill him and I'll have that on my conscience for the rest of my life. *Aren't* you?"

Now Mother is going to tell her son, icily, that he is contemptible. She has won, and as long as Phil insists on this technique Mother will always win. This is a sad way to spend your life—please don't do it. At the time it may feel wonderful, especially if you are someone who has heard Mother run through that particular speech hundreds of times already. But the end results aren't worth the two or three minutes of gratification. You are only reinforcing your mother in this pattern of verbal attack by demonstrating that it will work so well on you.

7

SECTION D ATTACKS:

"Even *You* Should . . ."

The most basic form of the Section D attack is anything but subtle and certainly should be hard to overlook. The very first word is "even," and the strong emphatic stress on whatever follows makes the fact that this is an attack unmistakable. Notice that just the two words "Even *you*," all by themselves, are perceived as an insult. If you try to think of some way to start a sentence with "Even *you*" and finish it without having insulted the person you're speaking to, you'll find it very hard to do. The only examples I can imagine are sorrowful statements of fact in Leveler Mode, such as "Even *you* forgot to write your paper!", where there is at least a hint that the speaker is surprised that someone like yourself would do that. And it still is far from complimentary. The basic pattern looks like this:

"Even [X] should [ought to; could: would: might: can; may; must; will] [Y]."

That long list of items with "should" at the top is the set of English terms called "modal auxiliaries." Like "even," they pack an astonishing amount of information into a very small space.

Here are some likely fillers for [X] and [Y]:

"**Even** *you* . . .

"**Even a** *woman* . . .

"**Even a** *first*-**grader** . . .

"**Even someone** *your* **age** . . . .

"**Even an** *uned*ucated **person** . . .

"**Even a** *law*yer . . .

. . . should . . .

be able to understand the basic facts of *life*."

appreciate the fact that *money* **doesn't grow on** *trees*."

know that term papers have to be *typed*."

realize that *smoking* **is bad for your** *health*."

be able to remember that *other* **people have rights** *too*."

As is true for all the VAPs, the exact placement of emphatic stresses in this attack can vary. For example, it can also appear with a heavy stress on one or both syllables of "even" as in "*Ev*en *you* . . ." and "*Ev*en someone *your* age . . .". The additional stresses increase the intensity of the attack and make it more hostile. Now let's pick one combined example and analyze it.

"**Even someone** *your* **age should know that term papers have to be** *typed*."

PRESUPPOSITIONS:

- "Whatever your age is, there's something wrong with being that age—it's not an age to be proud of."
- "The fact that term papers have to be typed is so well known that for you not to know it is further proof of how ignorant and inferior you are."
- "You should feel very guilty and ashamed."

YOUR PERSONAL OCTAGON

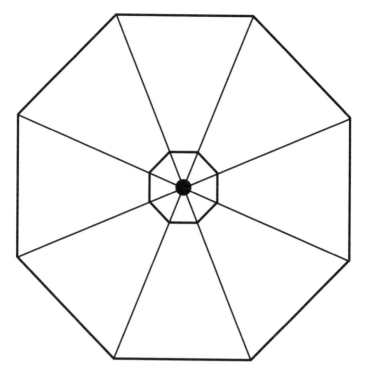

The worst possible response to this is to take the bait and start talking about term papers and the typing of term papers. Responses that are guaranteed to be losers go like this:

"I *always* type my papers! But my *computer* crashed, and it was Sunday and there wasn't any way to get it *fixed*, and the paper was due today, and today is *Mon*day!"

This will earn you a chilly lecture about waiting until the very last minute to type your papers, learning to plan ahead so that you never find yourself in a bind like that, and similar moralisms.

"I don't see why they have to be typed, as long as they're neat and easy to read."

You can't win with this one, because it's the teacher who sets up the requirements for paper format, not you. You are in the position of a speeder arguing with a police officer about what the speed limit ought to be.

"You never *said* papers had to be typed!"

Oops. If you want to be stomped on, this is a good way to guarantee it. The response will be "The reason I did not say that they had to be typed is because—as I have already pointed out to you—even someone *your* age should know that term papers have to be typed." Not only was it necessary to attack you verbally, you see, but it had to be done *twice*, in duplicate, in order to get through to you—and you helped.

Please don't do this. You can be absolutely positive that although you may not have known about whatever it was that filled the [Y] slot, it is something your opponent can get away with claiming that you have no excuse not to know about; otherwise, it wouldn't be appearing in this pattern. You are never going to hear a Section D attack in which [Y] is filled by something likely to be known only to specialists, such as "Even someone *your* age should know that Mount Erebus is just over thirteen thousand feet *high*."

When you're dealing with one of the verbal attacks on the Octagon, or any of the other English VAPs, your strategy is to ignore the bait, identify the hostile language sheltered in the presuppositions, and respond to that hostile language, not to the bait. Please look at the following sample confrontation.

CONFRONTATION EIGHT: *A HUSBAND & WIFE*

FRED: "Even a woman ought to be able to change a flat *tire*, you know!"

MIRIAM: "I *can* change a flat tire, and just as well as any *man* can, *too*!"

FRED: "Sweetheart, there's no need for that tone of voice, or that look on your face. Just because I want to be sure you don't find yourself stuck out on some highway in the middle of nowhere—"

MIRIAM: "Now *wait just a min*ute, here! What exactly do you mean by 'that tone of voice' and 'that look on your face,' *any*way? *You started* this, you know!"

FRED: [With a look of total amazement] "I did *what*??"

Miriam has no hope whatsoever and very shortly will be told at some length about how impossible it is to talk to her about anything, how touchy she is, and how she blows up over every little thing and imagines that Fred is trying to pick fights. And then she'll be apologizing and saying that she simply doesn't know what on earth is wrong with her. She should go to Computer Mode, respond to the hostile language in a presupposition, and maintain that stance, like this:

FRED: "Even a woman ought to be able to change a flat *tire*, you know!"

MIRIAM: "The idea that women are somehow inferior and help-less is rather common. I'm surprised to hear it coming from *you*, darling."

Miriam's utterance is in no way hostile, and will leave Fred with some intricate verbal maneuvering to do. It's gentle, and it ends with a compliment presupposing that Fred isn't the sort of unsatisfactory person who would have said what he said and that it must have been a slip. Perhaps *he* is not quite himself lately.

The worst choice that Miriam could make would be to coun-terattack with, for example, something along these lines:

MIRIAM: "The opinion that women are somehow inferior and ignorant is rather common in men *your* age, darling. I'm sorry to hear that you feel that way."

This is exactly like pouring gasoline on a fire, and is completely counterproductive. The essential pattern for an appropriate response to a Section D attack looks like this:

"The opinion that *(whatever is presupposed by [X])* **is rather** *(some appropriate adjective such as 'common' or 'interesting' or 'typical')*. **I am surprised to hear it from** *you*."

For example:

FRED: "Even a woman ought to be able to change a flat *tire*, you know!"

MIRIAM: "The idea that women are somehow inferior and helpless is rather common. I'm surprised to hear it from *you*, darling."

FRED: "Oh? And why is that?"

MIRIAM: "Because you're not the kind of person who says things like that."

FRED: "Oh."

Now let's move on to the practice confrontations for this chapter.

CONFRONTATION NINE: *A HOSPITAL PATIENT & A NURSE*

ELLEN JAMES: "Even a *nurse* should be able to tell that I'm *really* in a *lot* of *pain*!"

NURSE MARTIN: _____

_____

MS. JAMES: _____
_____
_____
_____
_____

NURSE MARTIN: _____
_____
_____
_____

CONFRONTATION TEN: *TWO FRIENDS*

CAITLIN: "Even someone who has no interest at *all* in other people's feelings ought to be willing to make an effort *once* in a while!"

LAURA: _____
_____
_____
_____

CAITLIN: _____
_____
_____
_____

LAURA: _____
_____
_____
_____

SECTION D ATTACKS ON ME

DATE _____

SITUATION _____

_____

_____

_____

(FIRST MOVE) **WHAT MY OPPONENT SAID**

_____

_____

_____

WHAT I SAID

_____

_____

_____

WHAT I SHOULD HAVE SAID

_____

_____

_____

(SECOND MOVE) **WHAT MY OPPONENT SAID**

_____

_____

_____

WHAT I SAID

_____

_____

_____

WHAT I SHOULD HAVE SAID

_____

_____

_____

(THIRD MOVE) WHAT MY OPPONENT SAID

_____

_____

_____

WHAT I SAID

_____

_____

_____

WHAT I SHOULD HAVE SAID

_____

_____

_____

(FOURTH MOVE) WHAT MY OPPONENT SAID

_____

_____

_____

WHAT I SAID

_____

_____

_____

WHAT I SHOULD HAVE SAID

_____

_____

_____

CONFRONTATION NINE

ELLEN JAMES: "Even a *nurse* should be able to tell that I'm *really* in a *lot* of *pain*!"

NURSE MARTIN: "You know, it's amazing how many people still feel, after all these years, that nurses have little or no training. What do you suppose accounts for that?"

MS. JAMES: "*Do* nurses get a lot of training?"

NURSE MARTIN: "Well, in this state we have to finish three whole years in a nursing education program. And then we have to pass a state examination."

The nurse is handling this well. With a patient who is in pain, winning or losing an argument isn't relevant, and Nurse Martin is keeping that in mind. The point is to reassure the patient, who may actually be afraid that the nurse doesn't know how to do anything useful and wants a doctor at once. If Ellen James *is* in pain (and the proper assumption should be that that's so, until there is evidence to the contrary), Nurse Martin is also helping with that problem. Distracting Ms. James with an abstract discussion of nursing training is useful here. If, while talking to her, the nurse also has to do unpleasant things with tubes or needles or other medical apparatus, distraction is all to the good.

ELLEN JAMES: "Even a *nurse* should be able to tell that I'm *really* in a *lot* of *pain*!"

NURSE MARTIN: "There's nothing wrong with being a nurse,

ma'am. Nurses are skilled professionals."

MS. JAMES: "Oh, yeah? I came in here hurting like the devil, and what you're doing hurts worse than what I came in with, and you either call a doctor right now or I'm walking out of this place before one of you 'professionals' finishes me off!"

NURSE MARTIN: "You're free to leave if you like, ma'am, but I do *not* have to listen to any more of your insults, and I don't intend to."

This is an unfortunate mess. People who are sick and in pain are not at their most reasonable to begin with, and nurses know that. This nurse is now in the middle of an undignified and unprofessional row with a patient, and whether the patient deserves it or not doesn't matter; it should not have happened.

The nurse was correct to respond to the presupposition that there's something wrong with being a nurse. But she has forgotten to respond with a *neutral* question or remark; there's nothing neutral about the move she made in response to Ms. James's Section D attack. If Ms. James doesn't happen to be a "skilled professional," it has gone beyond the level of nonneutrality and become an insult. Bad form, and nowhere to go but downhill. The patient will complain about this nurse, no matter how skillful and efficient the care provided may be, and the already low opinion she has of nurses in general has now been given a strong reinforcement that will be no help in the future.

ELLEN JAMES: "Even a *nurse* should be able to tell that I'm *really* in a *lot* of *pain*!"

NURSE MARTIN: "Ma'am, have you always thought that nurses don't really know what they're doing?"

MS. JAMES: "Look, are you insinuating that I was trying to insult you? Because if you *are*, you've picked the *wrong person* to try *that* with!"

NURSE MARTIN: "I was only trying to help, Ms. James. If I've offended you, I'm sorry."

This version is an example of using more force than the situation requires; the question Nurse Martin asks isn't really neutral. It comes too close to *accusing* Ms. James of having said that nurses don't know what they're doing. The fact that Ms. James's Section D attack has emphatic stress on four words in a single sentence is a clue: it suggests that she's in pain, that she's upset and frightened, and that she may be a bit touchy. For the nurse to switch to Placater Mode in an attempt to apologize is only going to make her even more uneasy.

It's a good idea to remember that most people who begin an utterance with "Even a *nurse*" are not contrasting nurses with all other possible sets of individuals in the universe. Usually what they mean is "Even a nurse" as compared with a doctor. The outdated traditional stereotype that has doctors carrying the power of life and death and nurses carrying bedpans is something that patients may not be aware they feel. It's strongly reinforced by images of doctors and nurses on television, in movies, and in written materials, starting with the first reading text in elementary school where the nurse is always a respectful female doing minor things to assist a forceful male doctor who is doing *important* things. Nurses still have to contend with this stereotype, and it might just as well be looked upon as one of life's burdens, along with heavy traffic and bad weather. Being defensive about it, even when fully justified, isn't going to help matters.

ELLEN JAMES: "Even a *nurse* should be able to tell that I'm *really* in a *lot* of *pain*!"

NURSE MARTIN: "You're absolutely right, and I'm going to do something about your discomfort just as quickly as possible."

MS. JAMES: "I'm sorry, Nurse—I guess I'm not being very pleasant."

NURSE MARTIN: "Anybody who's in pain is likely to be a little bit on edge. No problem."

In this example Nurse Martin has ignored the fact that the patient's opening utterance contained a presupposed insult and has agreed with it as if it had been made neutrally. (Whether a particular patient deserves this sort of treatment or is a chronically abusive person who needs no further encouragement of bad habits is a decision that has to be made for each individual case.) Ms. James has reacted politely, and Nurse Martin has not rubbed her nose in the apology. The immediate switch Nurse Martin made—from responding to the individual patient to using the abstract Computer Mode "anybody who's in pain"—was a skillful move. To have said back, "Oh, the only reason you insulted me is because you're in pain, and I don't pay any attention to that kind of thing" would have been much less skillful; it would have smacked of "Me, Noble Professional; you, Primitive Patient."

CONFRONTATION TEN

CAITLIN: "Even someone who has no interest at *all* in other people's feelings ought to be willing to make an effort *once* in a while!"

LAURA: "When did you start thinking I don't have any interest in other people's feelings?"

CAITLIN: "You *don't*. It's obvious to *any*body. The only thing *you* care about is your own *self*."

LAURA: "Like I said, when did you start feeling this way?"

Caitlin is determined to stay in Blamer Mode and is not going to be distracted from that intention by Laura's neutral question. Whatever it is that's bothering Caitlin is going to have to be brought out in the open eventually, and all Laura can do is hang in there. The chances are about 9 to 1 in a confrontation like this that shortly—if Laura can remain calm and neutral—Caitlin will bring up a specific incident: a forgotten birthday, for example, or a hurtful remark overheard somewhere or repeated to her by someone else. Something that has been festering and needs to be talked about. The goal, if Laura values the friendship, should be to find a way to get to Leveler Mode so that these two people can get to the bottom of the matter and be rid of it.

CAITLIN: "Even someone who has no interest at *all* in other people's feelings ought to be willing to make an effort *once* in a while!"

LAURA: "When did you start thinking I don't have any interest in other people's feelings?"

CAITLIN: "Yesterday. When I needed your help in that meeting, and you just sat there without saying a word and watched me go down the tubes."

LAURA: "Want to go get some coffee and talk about it?"

Laura, if she is paying close attention, will be facing a temptation here. The bait in this Section D has a presupposition that she *never* makes an effort to consider other people's feelings. Then here comes this single incident from yesterday, and the temptation will be strong to say something like "I thought you said I *never . . .*" and so on. If that happens, however, Caitlin will begin dredging up other incidents, valid or ridiculous, and these two people will be stuck in a Blamer/Blamer loop, headed nowhere. In a situation like this one, resist the temptation, and try to make the one incident the focus of your conversation.

What if your invitation for coffee and talk is turned down? What do you do? Just say, "Okay," and let it go. There'll be other chances to mend the fences if you want to mend them. Do not Placate; one invitation is enough, and a Placater response to Blaming is always a bad strategy.

CAITLIN: "Even someone who has no interest at *all* in other people's feelings ought to be willing to make an effort *once* in a while!"

LAURA: "Have you always felt that way about me? I thought we were *friends!*"

CAITLIN: "If we weren't friends, would I be bothering with this?"

LAURA: "Well, if it's such a bother, *don't!* The *last* thing I need is comments from you about *my char*acter!"

This is what usually happens when, as you're asking your question in response to a hostile presupposition, you can't resist throwing in a little something extra. Caitlin might have responded, "We *are* friends, and *no*, I haven't always felt this way," and so on into a productive discussion. On the other hand, things may go as in the example, and by throwing out that jab—"I thought we were *friends!*"—Laura is leaving the floor wide open for escalation of the attack. Notice the presupposition in the tag line: Caitlin will hear this line as "I thought we were friends, but obviously I was mistaken and you're *not* my friend." The heavy stress on "friends" in "I thought we were *friends!*" guarantees that.

8

SECTION E ATTACKS:

"Everyone Under*stands* Why You . . ."

There are two basic patterns for the Section E attack. The first uses the undefined term "everyone" and looks like this:

"Everyone under*stands* why you [X]."

Possible items to fill the [X] are:

    . . . are so emotional."

    . . . are so confused."

    . . . are so hysterical."

    . . . really haven't been your*self* lately."

    . . . can't bring your sales figures up to a normal level."

    . . . are having so much trouble adjusting to your situation."

The other basic pattern simply makes the "everyone" more specific, replacing it with a sequence that applies to a particular group, like this:

"All the other members of the staff under*stand* why you ..."

"Every student in this program under*stands* why you . . ."

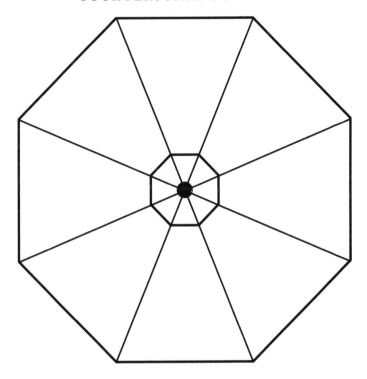

"**All of the men/women who have to work with you under-stand why you . . .**"

"**Every nurse on this floor under*stands* why you . . .**"

This opening is then followed by items filling [X], as in the simpler pattern.

It's also possible to throw many other frills into the mix, giving us such monstrosities as:

"**Everyone in this department with even a shred of common sense under*stands* why you are finding it so incredibly difficult to live up to our *stan*dards, Ms. Jones.**"

Here we have presuppositions piled and stacked and coming out of the woodwork. An attack like this can be extremely difficult to handle. This is particularly true because it often happens when you're alone with another person who may disguise a vicious attack with a facade of tender, loving concern for you. Section E VAPs may leave a novice feeling beaten and bewildered and unable to understand why he or she has reacted so strangely to this person who has just been so *kind*.

From your work with the earlier sections of the Octagon, you will be aware that the bait in this attack (the part to be ignored) is what appears on the surface and is designed to get your attention, filling the [X] slot in the pattern. You do not, under any circumstances, want to answer with replies like these:

"Anybody who is saying that I'm emotional is completely out of line, and I want that understood. In no *way* am I emotional!"

"What do you *mean*, 'everyone understands?' If there are people in this office talking about me and calling me names, I'm not surprised, but it's *those* people who have the problems, not *me*!"

Responses like these, even if they are absolutely true, even if you are an island of serene competence in a sea of chaos, are only going to sound as if you are—as you're claimed to be—emotional or unable to cope. Everything you say along these lines will get you in deeper and deeper.

Equally futile and foolish is an attempt to argue that you *can* meet your sales quotas or pass your exams or whatever it is being alleged in [X] that you're having trouble with. And this sort of futile foolishness is exactly what the person attacking you expects to hear from you.

Here are the presuppositions that go with a Section E attack:

"There is something very wrong with you."

"This 'something wrong' is well known to everyone around you."

"You should be very grateful to all of us for being so perceptive and so understanding."

"You should be very ashamed of yourself."

Section Es are based upon one fundamental truth: that everybody in the whole world has *something* he or she looks upon as a shameful secret and would hate for anyone else to know about. And anyone using a Section E attack, even with no idea at all what your secret is, can count on two things: the fact that *you* know what it is, and that your reaction to "Everyone under*stands* why you [X]" is almost certainly going to be "Oh, no! Everybody *knows* about it!"

I assure you that it's most unlikely that they do know about your personal secret. Whether it's your sexual preference or the fact that you once took three dollars from petty cash and have never put it back, that you were arrested nine years ago for running a red light, or—as in the vast majority of people I come across—just a conviction that your thighs are lumpy or that you're too short, makes no difference. True, if you've done something really awful, it may have come to light—but usually that is not the case. Usually the person using a Section E move against you is simply counting on you to fill in the secret yourself and fall apart about it.

I have seen a student, once or twice, fall right into this trap and blurt out something like "Oh, *no! How* did you find *out* that I cheated on the test?" when the instructor had never suspected anything of the kind. Don't do that, please. If you have something to confess, the time for confessing may come along later and you may have an ethical and moral decision to make about that. But this is *not* the time.

Which leads us to what you *can* safely do. There is a beginner's move that has a high safety factor and requires little effort. It will come as a great surprise to your attacker. Like this:

ATTACKER: "Everyone under*stands* why you [X]."

YOU: "How very kind of them. I'm deeply touched."

A response of this kind leaves your attacker in a curious position, if you do it properly. That is, if you sound sincere, calm, and mildly interested in what's coming next. You have now presupposed, you see, that you and the attacker and all the members of the mysterious "everyone" (or other specified group) share your secret. And if this person you're dealing with is working from ignorance, as is typical, he or she is going to have the communication problem now, not you. This defense is one you can memorize, just as you memorized "Pardon me" for when you bump into somebody. Use it, and then sit back and wait. Calmly.

More advanced versions of this defense are responses such as the following:

"A company [or department, or therapy group, or whatever] that is able to achieve a spirit of community such as that demonstrated by what you have just said to me is rare, and is a credit to your leadership. One can only feel sympathy for other groups in which that spirit is lacking."

You'll realize that except for the compliment about "your leadership" this is in Computer Mode. You'll recognize it as a response not to the bait but to the presuppositions, as a denial that you either feel or should feel any guilt (or any gratitude) other than a kind of neutrally polite appreciation of the group's good manners. It's going to be very hard to follow it up by saying something nasty back at you. Furthermore, you will recognize it as a move away from the personal and dangerous one-on-one situation that opened the exchange, toward a much safer discussion of an abstract issue—the "spirit of community" and its various ramifications. (If "spirit of community" isn't appropriate, by the way, insert whatever chunk of jargon does fit your situation.)

Your attacker has now been complimented by you at length. What may amaze you is how much of this you can lay on, and how thickly you can lay it on, without it being recognized for the shuck it is. People in power, especially people in power who enjoy using Section E moves, can swallow an incredible amount of this sort of thing if you keep it in Computer Mode, using personal language only when—as with "what you have just said to me"—it's absolutely necessary. How far you want to carry it depends on how strong your own stomach is and how skilled you are at judging your opponent's limits. The example above seems to me to go about as far as you should either need or want to go. However, it's important for you to be aware that the reaction to your response is not as likely to be that you're overdoing the compliments as you would think. The Section E user is often almost lusting to hear about his or her great abilities as a leader or scholar or administrator.

NOMINALIZATION

I want to introduce one concept here, very briefly, because it's such an important characteristic of rhetoric and has been used in the expanded defense move in this chapter. It's called *nominalization,* and its function in verbal encounters is to hide away whatever is actually being claimed. Obviously, for you to say to the Section E attacker, flatly and baldly, "You are a great leader," would be ludicrous. It wouldn't work, despite what you see happen in television sitcoms. (At least I hope it wouldn't; I hope nobody is that naive and still in a position to use Section Es on you.) But you do want to slip that remark in there, where your attacker will hear it without quite realizing where it came from. You do that by nominalization, with "your leadership." Look at these examples:

① **A.** "The students cheated on their final exam."

① **B.** "The students' cheating on their final exam distressed the entire faculty."

② **A.** "Elizabeth is careless with her credit cards."

② **B.** "Elizabeth's carelessness with her credits cards puzzles her family."

③ **A.** "Bob is cruel to animals."

③ **B.** "Bob's cruelty to animals is something that none of us who know and admire him can understand."

In each of the **(A)** examples a flat statement has been made, as an open and overt claim. The burden of its proof is on the speaker, and anyone listening can legitimately ask for that proof. In the **(B)** examples, however, those same claims have been nominalized and moved into subject position in the sentence, where they are now only presupposed. That is, "the students cheated" presupposes that the students exist and claims openly that they cheated. "The students' cheating distressed the faculty" presupposes the existence of the cheating, and claims only that the cheating distressed the faculty. This is an ancient technique of the political speech, the propaganda message, and the sales pitch, and you need to recognize it when it's coming at you, even when it goes by very fast.

Nominalization means only turning something verblike or adjective-like into something nounlike. Some words have special forms for this process in English. For example:

"careless" becomes "carelessness"

"abandon" becomes "abandonment"

"patriotic" becomes "patriotism"

"resign" becomes "resignation"

However, any English verb can be nominalized just by adding "ing" to it; any English adjective can be nominalized by adding "being" in front of it. Typically, a possessive marker of some kind also appears. The examples that follow should make this clear:

④ **A.** "Bill burned down the building."

④ **B.** "Bill's burning down the building was an accident."

⑤ **A.** "He smokes."

⑤ **B.** "His smoking came as a surprise to me."

⑥ **A.** "For anybody to cheat is unwise."

⑥ **B.** "Cheating is unwise."

In example 6B you will notice that there is no possessive marker such as "Bill's" or "his." The person or persons doing the cheating have been eliminated from the utterance completely, and the abstract *action*—cheating, meaning "somebody unidentified's (or various somebodies unidentifieds') cheating"—appears by itself as the nominalization. This is advanced Computer Mode and is used frequently to create slogans to either rally round or protest against, as the case may be.

The more nominalizations you are able to use, the more claims you will be able to hide away as presuppositions. In Computer Mode it should almost never be necessary for you to make *any* open claim that could be objected to; that's why Computers never seem to take a stand on any issue. They constantly nominalize and then use something completely innocuous to finish their sentence. This is a technique to be practiced until you feel absolutely at ease with it, and it's something you should watch for until it's impossible for anyone to slip a nominalization past you unnoticed. A nominalization of either kind can appear anywhere in a sentence in which any other nounlike element can appear. For example:

⑦ **A.** "I am impressed because you are such an excellent leader."

⑦ **B.** "I am impressed by your being such an excellent leader."

⑦ **C.** "I am impressed by your excellent leadership."

⑧ **A.** "We are surprised that you are shy."

⑧ **B.** "We are surprised at your being so shy."

⑧ **C.** "We are surprised by your shyness."

Here are our sample confrontations for this chapter. In working with them, you might want to try to use nominalizations whenever you can fit them in.

CONFRONTATION ELEVEN:
A SALES MANAGER & A SALESPERSON

[Note: For this confrontation, assume that the "secret" worrying the employee, a part-time salesperson, is her personal conviction that her co-workers respect her less because of her weight.]

DORIS RILEY: "Dear, everyone under*stands* why you are having so much trouble finding a place for yourself in this job. We really *do* understand."

SUSAN REED: _____

_____

_____

_____

MS. RILEY: _____

_____

_____

_____

SUSAN: _____

_____

_____

_____

CONFRONTATION TWELVE: *A DOCTOR & A PATIENT*

[Note: Try approaching this confrontation with different combinations of gender in mind.]

DOCTOR: "I want you to know that every one of the doctors you have seen—and that includes myself—under*stands* why you are so convinced that you have a physical disease instead of an emotional problem."

PATIENT: _____

_____

_____

_____

DOCTOR: _____

_____

_____

_____

PATIENT: _____

_____

_____

_____

SECTION E ATTACKS ON ME

DATE _____

SITUATION _____

_____

_____

_____

(FIRST MOVE) **WHAT MY OPPONENT SAID**

_____

_____

_____

WHAT I SAID

_____

_____

_____

WHAT I SHOULD HAVE SAID

_____

_____

_____

(SECOND MOVE) **WHAT MY OPPONENT SAID**

_____

_____

_____

WHAT I SAID

_____

_____

_____

WHAT I SHOULD HAVE SAID

_____
_____
_____

(THIRD MOVE) **WHAT MY OPPONENT SAID**

_____
_____
_____

WHAT I SAID

_____
_____
_____

WHAT I SHOULD HAVE SAID

_____
_____
_____

(FOURTH MOVE) **WHAT MY OPPONENT SAID**

_____
_____
_____

WHAT I SAID

_____
_____
_____

WHAT I SHOULD HAVE SAID

_____
_____
_____

SAMPLE SCRIPTS

CONFRONTATION ELEVEN

DORIS RILEY: "Dear, everyone under*stands* why you are having so much trouble finding a place for yourself in this job. We really *do* understand."

SUSAN REED: "How kind of everyone. I appreciate their concern."

MS. RILEY: "Well, it includes me too, you know. *I* understand, *too*."

SUSAN: "It's certainly gratifying to know that."

This is properly done. Now Ms. Riley is going to have to come right out and say what it is that "everyone" understands, or else take another approach entirely. And Susan should do nothing to help her out of this bind.

DORIS RILEY: "Dear, everyone under*stands* why you are having so much trouble finding a place for yourself in this job. We really *do* understand."

SUSAN REED: "That's not at all surprising. The team spirit here is obvious, and it's something for which you are to be congratulated."

MS. RILEY: "Well . . . thank you. I appreciate that."

SUSAN: "Not at all. I believe in giving credit where it is due."

Having been complimented three times in a row, Ms. Riley is going to sound foolish if her next move is an accusation or a complaint. Susan has handled this well.

DORIS RILEY: "Dear, everyone under*stands* why you are having so much trouble finding a place for yourself in this job. We really *do* understand."

SUSAN REED: "Just because I'm overweight, Ms. Riley, does *not* mean that I can't handle my job. Overweight people are just like any other kind of people—they're a little larger, *that's* all!"

MS. RILEY: "*Really,* dear, your touchiness about your weight surprises me. If you're so sensitive about it that you let it interfere with your job performance, don't you think you should pull yourself together and go on a diet?"

SUSAN: "I have *tried* that. I've tried every diet that's ever been invented, and none of them work! That's not the *point*! The point is that it's not fair for you to accuse me of being no good at my job just because I'm *overweight*!"

This is a disaster. For one thing, Susan Reed has now given her boss the complete details about where to jab in order to cause pain, something that Ms. Riley may not have had any knowledge about up to this point. For another, Susan is now wide open for a new attack—"If you *really* wanted to lose weight, you'd find a way to *do* that, like everybody else!"—and all that goes with that attack. If Ms. Riley is looking for a perfect target, she appears to have found one.

DORIS RILEY: "Dear, everyone under*stands* why you are having so much trouble finding a place for yourself in this job. We really *do* understand."

SUSAN REED: "How perceptive of them—and how nice of you to mention it."

130

MS. RILEY: "Well . . . . That's not really what I wanted to talk to you about."

SUSAN: "Oh, sorry. Nothing like a misunderstanding to start off a conversation! Why don't we start over?"

Susan has done this very skillfully and is now in as much command of the situation as is possible, given the fact that she is the employee and has little in the way of power to use against her boss. If Ms. Riley now moves to Blamer Mode and starts criticizing Susan's job performance—which is likely—she will do so on a footing of less dominance and will have to lay her cards openly on the table. No matter how things go from there, Susan has earned a few points. Notice, too, that by using the nominalization "a misunderstanding," Susan has avoided having to make any claim as to who misunderstood whom.

CONFRONTATION TWELVE

[In the examples that follow, all possible combinations of gender have been used for doctor and patient. This is because gender differences in doctor/patient interactions tend to have drastic effects.]

DR. FRED JONES: "I want you to know, Cleo, that every one of the doctors you have seen—and that includes myself—under*stands* why you are so firmly convinced that you have a physical disorder instead of an emotional problem."

CLEO FRENCH: "Do they? I'm sure the support of one's peers is always reassuring in situations of this kind, Doctor."

DR. JONES: "I'm not sure you understand what I was trying to say to you, Cleo."

CLEO: "That is of course possible." [Waits with an expression of neutral interest on her face.]

In this situation you cannot, as patient, express gratitude or appreciation for the doctor's statement, no matter how many other doctors agree with him. Since you *don't* agree, that would be absurd and would reinforce his conviction that you have emotional problems. The patient is probably at a number of disadvantages here: the doctor is dressed, while the patient is wearing only a sheet or a paper gown; the doctor is addressed by title, while the patient gets first-name treatment; the doctor is male, the patient is female; and so on. Under the circumstances, Cleo is well advised to go to Computer Mode and try to adjust the unequal dominance situation a bit, and that is what she has done. Dr. Jones is going to have to be more specific.

DR. FRED JONES: "I want you to know, Cleo, that every one of the doctors you have seen—and that includes myself—under*stands* why you are so firmly convinced that you have a physical disorder instead of an emotional problem."

HARRY BRANT: "The way doctors are always able to agree on every issue is amazing. You have to wonder what the medical profession would be like without that determination to hang together no matter what."

DR. JONES: "Oh, I think that impression of doctors is very much exaggerated."

HARRY: "Hmmm. Interesting."

So far, Harry is ahead. Dr. Jones has just questioned the idea that the consensus opinion of a group of doctors is necessarily inevitable, which is some distance away from the question of whether Harry's problem is physical or emotional. It's now the doctor's move, and he will have to pursue this unrelated topic, retrace his moves and begin again, or choose some totally different strategy. Whatever he decides, he's been thrown off course. Harry has maintained Computer Mode throughout the exchange and is in a strong position.

DR. REBECCA WEST: "I want you to know, Cleo, that every one of the doctors you have seen—and that includes myself—under*stands* why you are so firmly convinced that you have a physical disorder instead of an emotional problem."

CLEO FRENCH: "That's to be expected, under the circumstances; anticipating a *lack* of agreement would be unrealistic."

DR. WEST: "You're not surprised, then?"

CLEO: "If you *expected* me to be surprised, Doctor, that does surprise me. Perhaps I misunderstood your first remark."

Cleo is doing reasonably well here. She and the doctor are fencing, and where this may lead is impossible to predict. The first response she made, using the phrase "under the circumstances," was an excellent move. Dr. West has presupposed that everyone (that is, the set of doctors Cleo has seen) knows something about Cleo that justifies the claim Dr. West is making. Cleo has replied with an utterance presupposing that she knows something, too; with any luck at all, Dr. West is wondering what that is.

DR. REBECCA WEST: "I want you to know, Cleo, that every one of the doctors you have seen—and that includes myself—under*stands* why you are so firmly convinced that you have a physical disorder instead of an emotional problem."

HARRY BRANT: "Yeah? Well, I want *you* to know, Doctor, that I am damn sick and tired of hearing that. I've heard it from half a dozen men who called themselves doctors, and I thought maybe from a woman doctor I might at least get a different opening *line*, for crying out loud! Thanks for nothing, Doctor."

DR. WEST: "Harry, try to listen to me reasonably, would you? I'm *not* saying you're not sick, and I'm *not* saying your pain isn't real, and neither are the other doctors. We're simply trying to explain to you that your problem isn't the kind of thing that we can help you with."

HARRY: "And I am saying that all of you are wrong, Doctor. And if I have to go to a hundred doctors before I find one that *knows* something about practicing medicine, I will."

Harry is losing, of course, and can't win. It makes no difference whether he's right or wrong about his condition. He may very well be sitting there with a genuine organic disease that can and should be treated by his doctor—for example, a gallbladder that ought to be removed. It doesn't matter. His language behavior in this confrontation is only going to reinforce Dr. West's perception of him as an overemotional person with little self-control who trudges from doctor to doctor in search of one who will agree with his personal diagnosis. That may be unjust, and even dangerous to the patient, but it is the way things are.

Doctor/patient confrontations are a special case because of the privileged position and status that physicians have in English-speaking society, and because—unlike the situation in most confrontations—the doctor may well have the power of life and death, or at least the power to determine *quality* of life, with regard to the patient. This tends to create confrontations highly charged with overtones that would be absent in most other settings.

9

SECTION F ATTACKS:
"A Person Who . . ."

The Section F attack has an absurdly trivial-looking basic pattern. It goes like this:

"A person who [X] [Y]."

What makes this attack so dangerous is precisely those characteristics that make it look so boringly simple: it offers neither restrictions nor information. The pattern is in Computer Mode. It appears to refer only to some unknown "person." And almost anything can be used to fill [X] and [Y], making it a versatile attack that can turn up in almost any situation.

Here are some possible ways to fill the empty [X]:

"really **wanted to [Z] . . ."**

"has serious emotional problems . . ."

"doesn't even *care* **about [Z] . . ."**

"has limited perceptions . . ."

"has *no* **interest in anything** *mean***ingful . . ."**

Notice that this allows the stacking of attacks inside

attacks, and that a new empty slot can be put inside them with no difficulty at all. For example, we could fill [Z] in the third example like this:

"A person who doesn't even *care* **about his grades . . ."**

We can go on, using one example from the lists above, and look at some ways to fill term [Y] in the basic pattern. Like this:

"A person who *really* **wanted to pass this course . . .**

- **would be careful not to come in** *late* **every day."**
- **would** *never* **turn in a paper that hadn't been properly** re*searched* **and** *typed*.**"**
- **would do the assigned** *read*ing!"

If we now take just one of these examples and look at its primary presuppositions, we will have searched out most of the nooks and crannies of that innocent-looking "A person who [X] [Y]." Let's use this one:

"A person who *really* **wanted to pass this course would never turn in a paper that hadn't been properly re**searched **and** *typed*.**"**

The first presupposition that goes with this utterance is entirely a matter of logic: If there exists a person who really wants to pass this course, then that person would never turn in a paper that hadn't been properly researched and typed. However, if you are a student and the person who says this utterance is your instructor and is speaking directly to you, you know—from the circumstances and the context—that it contains three more presuppositions:

"There is a set of persons who really **want to pass this course—and you're not in that set."**

"Your paper wasn't properly researched."

YOUR PERSONAL OCTAGON

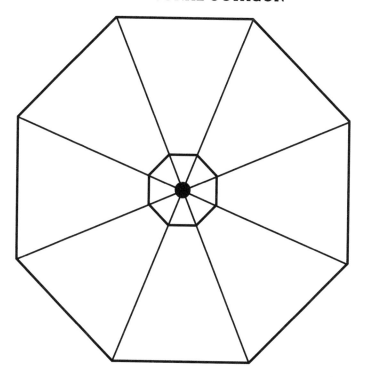

"Your paper wasn't properly typed."

The second and third presuppositions are the bait in this attack. But to take that bait and respond to it, with something along these lines:

"Dr. Garcia, I spent almost *six weeks* researching that paper, and it was typed according to the style sheet that you specified for the class *yourself*!"

is a bad move. You personally have *not* been openly accused of anything by the professor, who may very well inform you of that fact like this:

"Mr. Martin, I do not recall having even *mentioned* your paper, your research, or your typing."

That's devious, but it's accurate, and will make you look both conceited and foolish. Let's put this one through a few more moves.

CONFRONTATION 13: *A COLLEGE PROFESSOR & HIS STUDENT*

DR. GARCIA: "A person who really wanted to pass this course would *never* turn in a paper that hadn't been properly *researched* and *typed*."

HAL MARTIN: "Dr. Garcia, I spent almost *six weeks* researching that paper, and it was typed according to the style sheet that you specified for the class *yourself!*"

DR. GARCIA: "Mr. Martin, I do not recall having even *mentioned* your paper, your research, or your typing."

HAL: "But that's what you *meant!* I mean, you may not have said it right out in so many words, but that *is* what you *meant!*"

DR. GARCIA: "It's amazing how many students are convinced that they're able to read their professors' minds, Mr. Martin. To find you included in that group isn't particularly reassuring."

As you can see, Hal doesn't have a prayer. Nothing that he can say along this path will do anything but provide the professor with more opportunities to humiliate him. Hal has conceded by default that he doesn't really care anything about passing the course, and is busily engaged in proving that with every word that comes out of his mouth. He should extricate himself from this somehow, but doing it gracefully could be a major project. Just thanking Dr. Garcia for his time and fleeing is one of the most probable outcomes.

There are two ways to respond to a Section F attack without being trampled into the earth like the unfortunate Hal Martin. The first is one of those memorizable-for-emergency-use sequences, and it goes like this:

"That seems perfectly reasonable."

Think about this now. Someone has said to you that a person who really wanted to pass the course would do certain things. When you reply with "That seems perfectly reasonable," what have you accomplished?

Assuming that you've done this right, with neutral voice and other body language, you have rejected the possibility that you are the "person" being referred to. Since a Section F often depends on the attacker being able to maintain the position that he or she has never *claimed* you are that person, this goes a long way toward defusing the situation. Second, you, like your opponent, have made no reference whatsoever to your paper, your research, or your typing. Finally, you have—on the surface—agreed with every word being said to you. The professor now has two choices. He can switch to a much less impressive strategy and accuse you outright, like this:

"Then will you *please* explain to me why your paper is *abominably* researched and looks as if it had been *typed* by a *chipmunk*?"

Alternatively, the professor can move to a continuing abstract discussion of research and typing of papers by persons unknown and carry that on at any length he wishes. And Hal Martin should do precisely the same thing until escape becomes possible.

All of which brings us to an interesting and important point.

There are exceptions, of course, depending upon skill and context and many other real world factors. But as a basic rule of thumb, we can say the following: *with the single exception of Leveling, any language interaction between two individuals who are using the same Satir Mode will go nowhere useful.*

More individuals added to the group, also using the same Satir Mode, will only make things worse. That committees so often carry on their meetings entirely in Computer Mode is one reason why the work accomplished by committees often takes so long and is so minor in relation to the amount of energy and resources poured into the undertaking.

Placating at a Placater is an endless and undignified waste of time; Blaming at a Blamer always means a shouting match that degenerates into total futility; Distracting at a Distracter is panic feeding panic, and the result is chaos, not communication. Because both Blaming and Placating are hostile language behavior, any combination of those two modes also creates a hostility loop, and should be avoided. Two Computers talking to one another *sounds* better—and in fact, often sounds as if something significant were taking place—but very little actually happens; a Computing loop is a *dignified* delay.

One of the priceless survival skills in the academic world (and elsewhere, I suspect) is the ability to utter sequences in Computer Mode, within the field of discussion, for almost any length of time and at a moment's notice, without ever saying anything that has significant content. For example:

"There appears to be a significant probability, provided all parameters are maximized to their fullest potential within the constraints of demographic variance, that none of the anticipated data will demonstrate behavior atypical of that which one might encounter within the less constrained environment of either of the behavioral objectives, so to speak, or the derivationally motivated contingency. This is

of course somewhat oversimplified, but its implications need not be belabored, since they will be obvious to all of you, and you need only refer to the relevant literature (which, I might add, is abundant) for further details."

I put that together myself; I can go on like that without a pause for a very long time if need be. And so far as I know, if the sequence has any useful meaning at all, it's an accident. If I face an academic group and go through that sequence with a straight face, behaving as though I think it means something worth hearing, people will take notes, and they will nod wisely to indicate their agreement. And I would be absolutely delighted if someone raised a hand and said, "You know, I do not have the faintest idea what that means—if anything."

Learn a paragraph or two like the example above. If you can't construct them yourself, collect them from scholarly journals, and memorize them for future use. I'm quite serious about this. So long as they're sufficiently empty of content, you will be able to use them in any confrontation with someone who is using Computer Mode, and they will serve to fill up the time while you plan your next move.

Is there an appropriate response to a paragraph like mine, if you find yourself obligated to respond and don't want to bother providing another paragraph just like it? Yes, indeed. Look calm, raise your eyebrows ever so slightly, nod a very limited, polite nod, and say, "Except, of course, in the New Hebrides." Whatever follows "Except, of course" may be any time or place or situation or anything else you care to put there. "Except, of course, in the work of Gableframe-Soblowitz." "Except, of course, in the latter half of the rainy season." It makes no difference what you put there, and it will have one of two effects. To those who know that the original utterance was a put-on, it will be clear that you know that, too, and you will earn a status point and slide up in the pecking order a bit as someone who has to be watched out for. To those who have no idea that the original bit was anything but scholarly and profound, or was evidence of expert knowledge, *you* will appear to be scholarly and profound or expert. Neither outcome can do you any harm.

The jargon of the language environment you are functioning in must be acquired at once. Whether it's political science, bartending, military strategy, professional football, housewifery, surgery, or any of a multitude of other possibilities makes no difference. You need to learn the jargon, commit the list of essential words and phrases (meaningful or not) to memory, and begin using them with your peers. They are as crucial to your verbal self-defense as your hands and feet would be if you were learning karate; without them you are marked, *automatically*, as a potential verbal target.

At the beginning of this chapter I told you there were two possible ways to respond to a Section F attack. We have discussed the first; I would now like to take up the other possibility, and then close the chapter with your two practice confrontations. Please consider the following:

A: "A person who has serious emotional problems cannot possibly be expected to deal with the constant pressure and tension in this department."

B: "I couldn't agree with you more. The problem is, of course, deciding how a situation of this kind should be dealt with."

B's response, like "That seems perfectly reasonable," appears to be in full agreement with the attacker, and rejects the possibility that the speaker is the unidentified person under attack. But it raises the level of strategy by introducing a presupposition that not only are the two of you in agreement, but that you have in mind a particular person—not yourself—who the two of you agree has serious emotional problems, and so on. This is going to be awkward for your opponent, since you provide no way to determine who that person is, and asking you who it is would make your attacker look foolish. Let's see how this might play out.

KAREN LEE: "A person who has serious emotional problems cannot *possibly* be expected to deal with the constant pressure and tension in this department."

NORA WONG: "I couldn't agree with you more. The problem is, of course, deciding how a situation of this kind should be dealt with."

MS. LEE: [Lengthy silence.]

NORA: "You're quite right. There are no solutions that leap to the tip of one's tongue."

MS. LEE: "Well ... Ms. Wong ... what do *you* think ought to be the first step?" [Note: This is called *fishing*.]

NORA: "Frankly, the situation falls entirely outside my own area of expertise. That you called me in on the matter is gratifying, but I'm afraid you've overestimated the scope of my competence."

MS. LEE: "I see. Well, thank you, Ms. Wong."

NORA: "Not at all. I'm quite sure you'll find someone on the staff—or perhaps an outside expert—who will be able to clear things up satisfactorily."

This is an impressive performance on Nora's part. She has left her employer, who called her in to use a little verbal battery about her alleged "serious emotional problems," in a state of some confusion. Ms. Lee will be wondering whether some genuinely grave situation exists in the department, a situation that Nora—and perhaps everyone but Ms. Lee—knows about. This should distract her from Nora's hypothetical deficiencies for a while. It's not difficult to carry off a defense of this kind, I assure you; it just takes practice.

Now, here are your two practice sets.

CONFRONTATION 14: *A CAR SALESMAN & A CUSTOMER*

HUGH BLAKE: "A person who is genuinely concerned about the safety of his *family* would *never* buy one of those compact cars, sir. I tell you that from long experience."

SAM BARNHART: _____

_____

_____

_____

_____

HUGH: _____

_____

_____

_____

_____

SAM: _____

_____

_____

_____

_____

CONFRONTATION 15: *A HIGHWAY PATROLMAN & A DRIVER*

[Note: It's very common for the neutral "A person who" to be a more precise term in context, such as "A woman who" or "A minister who." This narrows the territory, but does not change the strategy.]

TROOPER GRANT: "A driver who has any concern for the lives and safety of *other* people on the road would *never* go weaving in and out of lanes at top speed!"

ARTHUR DREW: _____

_____

_____

_____

_____

TROOPER GRANT: _____

_____

_____

_____

ARTHUR: _____

_____

_____

_____

_____

SECTION F ATTACKS ON ME

DATE _____

SITUATION _____

_____

_____

_____

(FIRST MOVE) **WHAT MY OPPONENT SAID**

_____

_____

_____

WHAT I SAID

_____

_____

_____

WHAT I SHOULD HAVE SAID

_____

_____

_____

(SECOND MOVE) **WHAT MY OPPONENT SAID**

_____

_____

_____

WHAT I SAID

_____

_____

_____

WHAT I SHOULD HAVE SAID

_____

_____

_____

THIRD MOVE WHAT MY OPPONENT SAID

_____

_____

_____

WHAT I SAID

_____

_____

_____

WHAT I SHOULD HAVE SAID

_____

_____

_____

FOURTH MOVE WHAT MY OPPONENT SAID

_____

_____

_____

WHAT I SAID

_____

_____

_____

WHAT I SHOULD HAVE SAID

_____

_____

_____

HUGH BLAKE: "A person who is genuinely concerned about the safety of his *family* would never buy one of those compact cars, sir. I tell you that from long experience."

SAM BARNHART: "That seems perfectly reasonable."

HUGH: "Then you'll be wanting one of our *larger* models."

SAM: "No, I'll be buying one of the little ones, thanks."

Sam wins. For a salesperson to try to make a customer feel guilty by insinuating that he doesn't care if his family goes to a bloody or fiery death on the road is contemptible. It's none of Hugh's business how Sam feels about his family's safety, unless he has asked for advice on this matter. Hugh will be feeling foolish and frustrated at this point, and that's fine.

HUGH BLAKE: "A person who is genuinely concerned about the safety of his *family* would *never* buy one of those compact cars, sir. I tell you that from long experience."

SAM BARNHART: "I couldn't agree with you more. The problem, of course, is deciding whether to blame the automobile manufacturers, the government, or the advertising agencies."

HUGH: "Well, the *point* is that those little cars are death traps."

SAM: "The studies on the question of responsibility just don't get to the heart of the problem, as you are of course aware."

Pretty soon Hugh should catch on to the fact that Sam isn't going to play this game, and switch to some other strategy. Sam is winning.

HUGH BLAKE: "A person who is genuinely concerned about the safety of his *family* would never buy one of those compact cars, sir. I tell you that from long experience."

SAM BARNHART: "That seems perfectly reasonable to me. What doesn't seem reasonable is that—given your long experience—you're willing to *sell* those little death traps."

HUGH: "Now look—I only work here. I don't order the merchandise."

SAM: "I understand. Well, that must pose a serious ethical problem for you, since you have to sell a product you consider unsafe. How do you handle that?"

Game, set, and match to Sam. What is surprising here is the salesperson's lack of skill. Salespeople, especially professional full-time sellers of expensive items like cars and boats and motor homes, are ordinarily better trained in verbal interaction than the average person. Hugh's response was an amateurish mistake, and if the boss has heard it, he is going to be in trouble. He should have known better than to take Sam's bait.

HUGH BLAKE: "A person who is genuinely concerned about

the safety of his *family* would *never* buy one of those compact cars, sir. I tell you that from long experience."

SAM BARNHART: "You really mean that? I *do* care about my family's safety, and I don't intend to take any chances, if you know what I mean."

HUGH: "I tell you—the company has to provide what the public wants, and a lot of the public wants compact cars. But I wouldn't risk *my* family in one, and I'm glad to see that you're the kind of person who has better sense than to just go along with the herd."

SAM: "Well . . . It's a lot of money, and I was hoping for something with better mileage. But if it's a matter of *safety*, that's got to come first."

Hugh has won, and Sam hasn't even put up a mild struggle. Notice, too, that in Hugh's second move the responsibility for the product claimed to be unsafe has been skillfully dropped on the unthinking public. This, by contrast with the previous example, is what he is *supposed* to do.

CONFRONTATION 15

TROOPER GRANT: "A driver who has any concern for the lives and safety of *other* people on the road would *never* go weaving in and out of lanes at top speed!"

ARTHUR DREW: "That seems perfectly reasonable."

TROOPER GRANT: "Then why did you do it?"

ARTHUR: "I'm sorry, officer, I don't know—and I don't intend to do it ever again."

Like doctor/patient confrontations, those between law enforcement personnel and alleged breakers of the law are slightly different from ordinary arguments. The driver doesn't necessarily want to win this one; on the other hand, it's not necessary for him to grovel. The example seems to me to show the proper degree of respect for the officer and no more than that.

TROOPER GRANT: "A driver who has any concern for the lives and safety of *other* people on the road would *never* go weaving in and out of lanes at top speed!"

ARTHUR DREW: "What makes you think I don't have any concern for other people's safety, officer?"

TROOPER GRANT: "I don't believe this. What makes me think so? I *told* you—those lane changes you just made!"

ARTHUR: "Oh. Yeah."

Trooper Grant is right; he did explain exactly why he thought Arthur Drew's intention was to run everybody else off the road. This is no time to ask him to repeat it, whether Arthur agrees with him or not.

TROOPER GRANT: "A driver who has any concern for the lives and safety of *other* people on the road would *never* go weaving in and out of lanes at top speed!"

ARTHUR DREW: "You're absolutely right. The problem is, of course, what to do in a situation like that."

TROOPER GRANT: "A situation like *what*?"

ARTHUR: "Well, you have a truck bearing down on your bumper from behind, and another truck right in front of you going thirty-five up a hill, and neither one of them seems to know you're there. It's hard to know what to do in a case like that."

Arthur is doing fine here; and provided that he really was in a situation where some otherwise dangerous lane changes seemed to be the only choice available, this is a good way to approach the discussion. He has begun by agreeing with the officer. This should earn him a few points. Furthermore, he has managed to shift the discussion just a bit toward the question of lane-change strategies in general. Well done.

TROOPER GRANT: "A driver who has any concern for the lives and safety of *other* people on the road would *never* go weaving in and out of lanes at top speed!"

ARTHUR DREW: "You may be right, but let me tell *you*, officer, I was really in a *bind* back there! I notice you saw *me* changing lanes . . . How about the guy that was running me off the damned *road*? How come you aren't stopping *him*?"

TROOPER GRANT: "My, *you're* a polite one, *aren't* you? You have anything else to tell me about how you think I should do my job?"

ARTHUR: "Yeah, as a matter of fact I *do*. My taxes pay your *salary*, you know!"

I assume no comment is needed here. If you are looking for a strategy to use in confrontations with law enforcement personnel that will guarantee you an expensive ticket, talking to them in Blamer Mode like this is a good choice. Arthur Drew cannot possibly win.

10

SECTION G ATTACKS:

"Why Don't You Ever . . ."

You will immediately recognize the Section G pattern as an attack in Blamer Mode and as one that can be flipped tidily to a positive *"Why* do you *always* . . ."* version. The basic patterns are:

"Why **don't you ever [X]?"**

"Why **do you always [X]?"**

This VAP can occur with varying degrees of strong emphatic stress on "why." The stronger that emphasis on "why" is, the more strongly it presupposes "Whatever your reason is, I want you to know in advance that it's not good enough," and the more intensely hostile the attack is. Almost anything can be fit into the [X] term of the pattern. For example:

"Why **don't you ever . . .**

- **try to make me happy?"**

- **consider anybody's feelings but your own?"**

- **act like** *other* **people's mothers?"**

- want anybody *else* to have any fun?"
- think about the way your behavior affects the *other* people in this department?"

"*Why* do you always . . .

- get such a *kick* out of seeing me *mis*erable?"
- try to make me look *stu*pid?"
- knock yourself out to *ruin* things for everybody?"
- deliberately *humili*ate me in every way you can *think* of?"
- eat *so much junk* food?"

YOUR PERSONAL OCTAGON

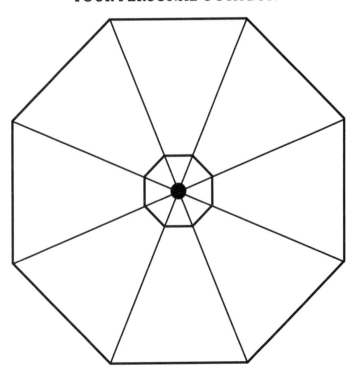

The presupposition of the Section G attack that's relevant for verbal self-defense is simply "You never [X]" or "You always [X]." It is certainly neither subtle nor complicated. Why, then, have I put it all the way up at the G level in difficulty instead of letting it share bottom rank with "If you *really* . . ."? Obviously it's not here because it offers levels of well-hidden interacting presuppositions that require great skill to disentangle. The problems with the Section G attack that make it so dangerous are these:

(1) Most of them come at you from people who, because you are involved in a close relationship with them, have real power to cause you pain. Unlike the teacher you see for only one semester or the mechanic you take your car to only once, people who come at you with Section Gs tend to be people with whom you spend large portions of your life. You can't say to yourself, "Oh, well, it's only a few weeks and then I'll never have to go near this person for the rest of my life." Because Section Gs so often have their source in people you must interact with constantly, they're troublesome.

(2) Leading right from the first problem is the fact that people in a position to try a Section G on you usually know your most vulnerable spots. If you worry because you think you're too thin or too fat, or because you didn't finish high school, or because your finances are in a mess, these people probably know about that. They may have been around you for years, and as a result they know *exactly* where to put the verbal knife.

(3) Because the Section Gs tend to be so personal and so vicious, they face you with a tremendous temptation to respond by hurting back. That is, you're likely to know as much about your attacker's weak spots as he or she does about yours. And in a sort of blind reaction to pain and rage you're likely to

take the bait, go straight to Blamer Mode yourself, and head into a full-scale shouting match filled with things that can never really be forgotten even though they may be forgiven. And if you have become highly skilled at verbal self-defense, you may even do harm for which you'll find it very hard to forgive your*self*.

These three factors, taken together, seem to me to cause Section G VAPs to merit the next-to-the-top spot in the ranking of difficulty, or even the very top spot. If you value—or badly need—the relationship you have with a Section G opponent, you *must* not give in to the temptation to hurt back. That can't end well; it's two primitives battering one another with boulders, and it has no possible good outcomes. If you *don't* value or need the relationship, of course, things are very different, and your best strategy is perhaps just to leave.

Trying to argue against the accusation doesn't help. It will go like this:

X: *"Why* don't you ever try to make *me* happy?"

YOU: "Sweetheart, I *do* try to make you happy!"

X: *"When?* Just tell me *one time* you did that!"

YOU: "Well, don't you remember the time that I . . ." [And here you insert your example, or your list of examples, and you will feel silly doing it.]

If you bring up the time you bought a Chevrolet instead of a Jaguar because you knew that X didn't want a Jaguar, you'll hear that the only reason you did that was because the Chevy was cheaper and furthermore you've never stopped rubbing X's nose in *that* one. If you bring up the time you gave up a trip to San Francisco at company expense because X couldn't go and therefore didn't want *you* to go, you'll hear that the real reason you did that was to have the satisfaction of telling everybody how narrow-minded X is and hearing them laugh about it. It won't get better—it will go on like that. For every token you offer, every shred of your evidence that you have tried many times to make X happy, X will have an alternative explanation that fits the picture of the world where all your energies are devoted to making X miserable. As your shreds of proof grow more trivial, you will feel more and more ridiculous. You should never start one of these absurd lists; that approach went out with gallant knights bringing fair maidens one token after another to be contemptuously rejected. "Remember the time I went out and killed nine giants with a single blow and brought you back their heads?" This back-and-forth is a cultural *script* that every native speaker of American English knows by heart and should rigorously avoid.

An effective nonhostile response to this Section G attack is one in which you do the following: *You immediately say something which, in itself, disproves the claim your attacker is making.* Preferably by offering something you can be sure that he or she doesn't want. For example:

HUSBAND: *"Why* don't you ever try to make *me* happy?"

WIFE: "Sweetheart, do you think maybe you'd be happier if we both quit our jobs and we moved to Wyoming?"

The sequence looks simpleminded, I agree. But this attack itself is simpleminded, and it deserves an equally simpleminded response, not a subtle one. The husband has claimed that his wife never does anything to try to make him happy. Immediately, without a second's delay, she proves that claim false; her response is an attempt to make him happy. The fact that it's outrageous has no relevance here. In fact, it may well be that the more outrageous it is, the better, so long as it doesn't make the husband feel that he's being made fun of. Especially if he's strongly opposed to what his wife is offering, it should cause him to drop the attack and devote his energies to heading off the offer. Above all, it will head off the list of proofs from the past, each of which he intended to painstakingly expose as not a genuine attempt to make him happy. This is what matters most of all. Let's try carrying this out for a few moves.

CONFRONTATION 16: *A HUSBAND & WIFE*

LARRY: *"Why* don't you ever try to make *me* happy?"

CYNTHIA: "Sweetheart, do you think maybe you'd be happier if we both quit our jobs and we moved to Wyoming?"

LARRY: [Stunned silence]

CYNTHIA: "Honey? Would you like that?"

LARRY: "The last thing on this *earth* I would ever want is for us to quit our jobs and move to Wyoming!"

CYNTHIA: "Well, then, let's not. I'm perfectly content with the way things are."

LARRY: "Move to Wyoming . . . . Pheeeeeew."

CYNTHIA: "Since that's settled, what would you like to do for dinner tonight?"

If something like that happens every time Larry tries Section Gs of this kind, he will give them up. They're no fun at all if the other person involved won't play the game and follow the script. They're rewarding only if they allow a long wallow in past regrets, broken promises, inadequate compromises, and all the rest of it. If they are instantly refuted with an offer like the one in Confrontation Sixteen, it will eventually become clear to Larry that this strategy is never going to pay off.

Section Gs should be looked upon as a bad habit to be broken, like scratching in public. They should be a habit you can break other people of reasonably quickly, by taking all the fun out of them. If you can't do that—if the other individual persists in spite of months of your best efforts—then you don't need verbal self-defense, you need an expert to find out what's wrong with that person or what's wrong with your relationship.

Once in a while a Section G will come your way from someone who isn't particularly close to you. You may just happen to have a boss who is a natural bully and enjoys the Blamer role. If you let this get to you and make you miserable, it's dangerous to your health and well-being. However, it can be handled in the same way it was in Confrontation Sixteen. For example:

CONFRONTATION 17: *YOUR BOSS & YOU*

BOSS: *"Why* don't you ever, even once, consider the feelings of the *other* people in this office and try to do something that would make life pleasanter for *them*, instead of thinking only of your*self*?"

YOU: "Okay . . . . How about if all the coffee breaks were thirty minutes instead of fifteen. I think that might do it."

BOSS: "Thirty-minute coffee breaks? You're out of your *mind!* We'd *never* get any work done around here!"

YOU: "Well, you're the boss. It's up to you."

Just be sure you pick something that the boss would never under any circumstances consider doing, but which will stand, in itself, as a refutation of the accusation. The principle is the same as in Confrontation Sixteen, but the stakes are lower. Getting a different boss may be difficult, but it's easier than getting a different spouse. Now, here are your practice confrontations, with sample scripts at the end of the chapter.

CONFRONTATION 18: *A TEENAGER & HER MOTHER*

ABBY: *"Why* do you *al*ways have to be *diff*erent? *Why* can't you act like *other* people's moms?"

MOM: _____
_____
_____
_____

ABBY: _____
_____
_____
_____

MOM: _____
_____
_____
_____

ABBY: _____
_____
_____
_____

MOM: _____
_____
_____
_____

HELEN: "*Why* do you al*ways* go out of your way to make me look *stu*pid and *ig*norant in front of all your friends? *Why* don't you ever let me have a chance to show people that *I* have a brain, *too*?"

LEO: _____

_____

_____

_____

HELEN: _____

_____

_____

_____

LEO: _____

_____

_____

_____

HELEN: _____

_____

_____

_____

LEO: _____

_____

_____

_____

SECTION G ATTACKS ON ME

DATE _____

SITUATION _____

_____

_____

_____

(FIRST MOVE) **WHAT MY OPPONENT SAID**

_____

_____

_____

WHAT I SAID

_____

_____

_____

WHAT I SHOULD HAVE SAID

_____

_____

_____

(SECOND MOVE) **WHAT MY OPPONENT SAID**

_____

_____

_____

WHAT I SAID

_____

_____

_____

WHAT I SHOULD HAVE SAID

_____

_____

_____

(THIRD MOVE) **WHAT MY OPPONENT SAID**

_____

_____

_____

WHAT I SAID

_____

_____

_____

WHAT I SHOULD HAVE SAID

_____

_____

_____

(FOURTH MOVE) **WHAT MY OPPONENT SAID**

_____

_____

_____

WHAT I SAID

_____

_____

_____

WHAT I SHOULD HAVE SAID

_____

_____

_____

SAMPLE SCRIPTS

CONFRONTATION 18

ABBY: *"Why* do you *always* have to be *diff*erent? *Why* can't you act like *other* people's moms?"

MOM: "Okay. From now on, like other moms, I'm giving you a ten o'clock curfew on school nights.

ABBY: "But, *Mom—*"

MOM: "And like other moms, I'll expect you to be in by eleven on Saturday night. Does that solve your problem?"

ABBY: "That's not fair!"

MOM: "Really? Let me introduce you, my dear, to the real world, in which *many* things are not fair. Including lots of other people's mothers."

It's true that this move on Mom's part immediately makes false the claim that she is never like other mothers and does it by offering something she's certain her daughter doesn't want. This is in full agreement with the instructions for responding to a Section G attack, and it may have been called for, depending on the daughter in question. However, there's no winner here, and no good outcome. Abby feels resentful, and if in fact she didn't deserve this she has been smacked down as surely as if her mother had used an open hand—and she won't forget it. The injury will fester. Mother feels smug right now, especially after the very witty finish line, but may well feel ashamed of herself later. What Mother has accomplished in this example is the teaching of a lesson: do not try being a Blamer at *me*, because I am more powerful than you are and I will see to it that you regret it. This may be temporarily satisfying, but it has two guaranteed effects: it will reinforce Abby's tendencies to use Blamer Mode, and it will create a serious communication breakdown with Abby, who'll go practice her Blaming on someone her own size in the future.

ABBY: *"Why* do you *always* have to be *diff*erent? *Why* can't you act like *other* people's moms?"

MOM: "Well, let's see. Would I seem more like other moms to you, honey, if I always waited up for you when you go out at night? And then you could come sit on my bed when you got home, and we could have a nice cozy chat about what your date was like, and what everybody was wearing . . . *You* know, *girl* talk. Would you like that?"

ABBY: "Mom, that would be *horrible.*"

MOM: "Well, then, we certainly don't have to do it."

Much better, and no further moves needed. If the after-date custom Mom described is already observed in this household, and enjoyed by both mother and daughter, it's not an option, and something else will have to be offered instead. On the other hand, it fits perfectly into the traditional image of the Devoted and Caring Mother Like Other Mothers and is an instant offer— which the Blaming daughter has to accept or turn down. Mom wins, without turning into a heavy parent figure, and without much effort.

Mom has to be careful not to overdo this, however, so that Abby won't think she is being made fun of. If "nice cozy chat" won't get by this daughter, Mom can pare it back to "a discussion of your evening." It has to be played absolutely straight.

ABBY: *"Why* do you *always* have to be *different? Why* can't you act like *other* people's moms?"

MOM: "I'm different from other moms? Hmmmm. How about if I cut my hair and quit wearing jeans?"

ABBY: "That wasn't the kind of thing I meant!"

Mom: "You don't want me to look like other mothers?"

ABBY: "No! I *like* the way you look!"

MOM: "Well, then, I don't think I understand. You want to talk about it a while?"

As with the move to Wyoming, Mom should be sure the offer she makes is either something she's willing to do or something Abby will be certain to refuse. In this sample script the mother has refused the "you're never like other moms" presupposition. She has done it immediately, without resorting to any Blaming. And she has led the confrontation to a point where a potential now exists for some productive Leveling.

ABBY: *"Why* do you *always* have to be *different? Why* can't you act like *other* people's moms?"

MOM: "Because *you* don't act like other *daught*ers, *that's* why! And until you do, I don't intend to put myself out for you."

ABBY: "Thanks a lot, Mother. I'll try to keep that in mind."

MOM: "You do that. And if you find yourself forgetting it, try another smart crack and I'll help you remember."

ABBY: "Thanks—I won't need any help."

MOM: "You're quite welcome. Drop in and have a little chat *any*time."

Very, very bad. Here we have two Blamers, whacking away at each other, using both fang and claw. The mother is serving superbly as a role model in this example, training her daughter in all the finer nuances of being an adult Blamer. She'll regret it eventually, and nobody wins.

CONFRONTATION 19

HELEN: *"Why* do you *always* go out of your way to make me look st*u*pid and *i*gnorant in front of all your friends? *Why* don't you ever let me have a chance to show people that *I* have a brain, *too*?"

LEO: "Okay, sweetheart. Next time the subject of oil depletion allowances comes up, *you* handle it."

HELEN: "You're *still* doing it!"

LEO: "Doing *what*?"

HELEN: "You know *perfectly well* what!"

LEO: "Sorry. You've lost me."

If this is a typical sample of Leo's language behavior, he too appears to be a chronic verbal abuser, and Helen is getting nowhere with the problem of finding a way to defend herself. He has responded with an immediate offer to show people that she, too, can shine in conversation and has carefully chosen something that he knows she doesn't want. But he has also carefully chosen something he is fully aware that she knows nothing about, and by doing so has (as she points out) demonstrated to her yet one more time how stupid and ignorant he can make her look and sound. She then goes right on Blaming, while Leo enjoys himself at her expense. Total silence would be less of a waste of time.

HELEN: "*Why* do you *al*ways go out of your way to make me look *stu*pid and *ig*norant in front of all your friends? *Why* don't you ever let me have a chance to show people that *I* have a brain, *too*?"

LEO: "Okay, sweetheart. How about if we give a big party—I mean a *really* big party—and we ask everybody we usually see around, and whoever else you'd like to invite. And I promise to keep my big mouth *shut* and let *you* do the talking."

HELEN: "Oh, dear . . ."

LEO: "Look, I wouldn't mind doing that at all."

HELEN: "I hate parties. Especially *big* parties."

LEO: "Then we don't have to do it. It was just an idea."

Very well done. Leo needs to demonstrate to Helen that the Section G move isn't a productive way to talk about things, and he's done that. At the same time, he's made her an offer that could plausibly fit into what she was asking him for, choosing something he could be sure she wouldn't want to accept. And of course he closes by reassuring her that he's not about to insist on her doing something she'd rather not do. It will be hard for Helen to find anything to complain about here.

HELEN: "*Why* do you *al*ways go out of your way to make me look *stu*pid and *ig*norant in front of all your friends? *Why* don't you ever let me have a chance to show people that *I* have a brain, *too*?"

LEO: "Because, my sweet, you aren't able to hold up your end of a conversation on any subject except diets and toilet training."

HELEN: "Your friends could use some current information on *both* of those topics!"

LEO: "You know what you *deserve*? You *deserve* for me to *let* you make a fool of yourself!"

HELEN: "Does it make you feel important, *talking* to me like that? Do you *enjoy doing that to me*?"

LEO: [Deep sigh] "If you *really* wanted to look intelligent, darling, *you'd* make an effort to learn something *worth talking* about!"

The only difference between Helen's language behavior here and in the first sample script is that she has learned to do her Blaming with a bit more sophistication. The only result is that Leo will feel free to return the ball with more force. Notice that he's now headed straight into a different verbal attack and is becoming more abusive with every move. This is a hopeless mess.

HELEN: "*Why* do you *al*ways go out of your way to make me look *stu*pid and *ig*norant in front of all your friends? *Why* don't you ever let me have a chance to show people that *I* have a brain, *too*?"

LEO: "You know, if I'm doing that, I should be ashamed of myself. Tell you what. You pick out a list of things you'd like to talk about next time we go out, and I'll promise to stay clear away from every one of them. Fair enough?"

HELEN: "No! Then I'd *really* look silly!"

LEO: "Why? Isn't that what you *wanted*?"

HELEN: "No! That's not what I meant at *all*. It would be obvious . . . and phony . . . and . . ."

LEO: "Well, look—do you want to stop someplace for coffee and *talk about this*? I don't seem to be getting the message."

This is well handled. The first offer Leo makes is sufficiently strange that it's not likely to be accepted, but it qualifies as doing what Helen says he never does. And it doesn't humiliate her or blame her, so long as he is careful to maintain a neutral stance and sound entirely serious. If Helen takes him up on his offer to talk it over, they may be able to do some Leveling and accomplish something useful. If she doesn't, he has at least headed off the argument. Leo is the winner, and is definitely not encouraging Helen to make a habit of using Blamer Mode for working out their difficulties. That's the primary goal, and he's following through properly.

11

SECTION H ATTACKS:

"Some [Xs] Would . . ."

We are now at the last of the attacks on the Octagon—Section H. Its basic pattern looks like this:

"Some [Xs] would [Y] if/when [Z] [W]."

We have a lot of unfilled terms there, each with its own potential for trouble. Because it would be confusing to take up the empty pieces one at a time, a sample with everything filled in is a good way to begin. Like this:

"Some instructors would really get angry if a student asked three stupid questions in a row!"

If we label the parts in that example to match the pattern above, the breakdown will look like this:

"Some . . .

    [Xs] instructors would

        [Y] really get *angry* if

            [Z] a student

                [W] asked three stupid questions in a *row*!"

The heavy stress on the word "some" at the beginning is important. As is often the case with emphatic stress, deleting it changes the meaning of the utterance—which means that its presuppositions will be different. Without the heavy stresses this sequence of words is not a Section H attack; it's just a neutral statement of an opinion.

Possible ways to fill in each of the empty terms should now be easier to follow. We'll go straight down the line.

"Some [Xs] . . .

- **wives; bosses; kids; patients; people; lawyers**

would [Y]

- **really not be able to under*stand***
- **resent it very *much***
- **really get *mad***
- **be absolutely *shocked***
- **not put up with it for *one* minute**

when/if [Z]

- **you**
- **a student**
- **a customer**
- **somebody who ought to know better**

[W]

- **always came to class *late* with a ridiculous ex*cuse*."**
- **was unemployed for the second time in one year."**
- **never could find time to talk for more than *five minutes.***"

[X] can be any set of individuals that the speaker can identify himself or herself as a member of. [Z] can be filled by anything at all that the speaker cares to use to represent the person spoken to—and it may very well contain within it other attacks from the Octagon. For example, [Z] may turn up as "a person who doesn't

YOUR PERSONAL OCTAGON

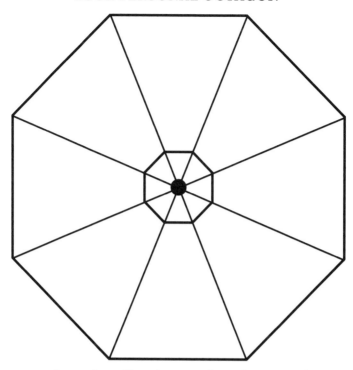

even *care* about the effect her smoking has on other people around her." Or worse.

Deep water, agreed? However, despite the pileup of possibilities here, and the potential for intricate presuppositions nested inside other presuppositions, there's nothing *new*. It's just a matter of carefully breaking the big pieces apart into smaller pieces and proceeding with each of them separately. The difficulty in the real world is, of course, that you have to do this in your head, very quickly, without getting mixed up. I suggest lots of practice and plenty of work in your journal. Working your way in writing through a dozen hypothetical Section H attacks, so that you can spend all the time you need thinking about them, will pay off the first time you find yourself facing a real one with about five seconds lead time.

Let's go back to the first example sentence in this chapter—"*Some* instructors would really get *ang*ry if a student asked three stupid questions in a *row!*"—and list its relevant presuppositions:

① You have asked three stupid questions in a row.

② Some instructors exist who, after three stupid questions from a student in a row, would really get angry.

③ I'm not *like* other instructors; I'm unique and superior.

④ You should feel very guilty and ashamed about your three questions.

⑤ You should feel very grateful to *me*, your unique and superior instructor.

When your instructor says that sentence directly to you, all of that content most assuredly is in there. And often there's a good deal more, depending on the particular situation; for instance, there may be a presupposition that the speaker has the authority and power to let you do something or keep you from doing something.

When a Section H attack is done well, it will be in Computer Mode throughout, with very few emphatic stresses or none at all. If the person using it fills term [Z] with the word "you"—as in "*Some* bosses would really get *mad* if you . . ."—that is an indication of little or no skill. The bait is whatever turns up in [W], and it should be ignored, like the bait in any other attack. If you take the bait, you will lose. Period. You cannot take the bait and win, no matter how satisfying it may be to surge into battle against this inexcusable accusation and shout your outrage and so on. You may enjoy that for a few minutes, but you will lose. Any time you take the bait in an attack and provide the attacker with the fight that he or she wanted, the attacker has won, no matter what else happens.

I have two suggestions for your response to a Section H attack. The first is more personal than the second; neither one is hostile, and either will do the job. Your choice depends on how pleasant you care to be to this person. Remember your basic pattern: *Some* persons [identified by your opponent] would react in a particular way to what you are claimed to be doing. That's what you will hear. And you should respond like this:

"Really? It would be interesting to hear your opinion on the matter, darling." [Or "Mr. White" or "Dr. Dayton" or whatever is appropriate.]

This is a skilled move. First of all, it blandly denies the most crucial of the presuppositions; as in the "a person who . . ." attack, it rejects the possibility that you are the individual being referred to in [Z]. Since your attacker hasn't said that you *are* that person, he or she has only been agreed with on a neutral abstract statement about opinions or reactions that some hypothetical person(s) might have. You haven't taken the bait. Furthermore, you have complimented your attacker by asking for his or her opinion, even though you know quite well that you've already heard it. You now have your Section H attacker in a tidy bind.

An alternative response, if you don't care much about your relationship with this person, is this one:

"That's genuinely interesting."

Now *wait*, looking very calm and only mildly interested. This is a Computer Mode response. It accomplishes the goal of removing you personally from the confrontation and rejecting the idea that you are involved. It uses the word "interesting" to refer to what's just been said, because in English "interesting" is the adjective you use when you don't want to commit yourself to being either for or against something. If a friend asks whether you like the poem she has just written, and you despise it, but you either don't feel competent to judge it or don't want to hurt her feelings, you say that it is "interesting."

There are two reactions that are almost universal in my workshops and seminars at this point:

"There's got to be some other way of doing it—that absolutely would not work."

Or:

"I could not possibly say either one of those things. No way. Other people could, maybe, but not me. I couldn't do it."

But I am obliged to tell you that making changes in those two responses will change the degree of challenge in your move, and may introduce new presuppositions that you didn't intend to include and that you may not be aware of—or both. The suggested responses will work, and they should not be tinkered with until you are highly skilled. If they sound phony and pretentious to you, that's all right. The Section H attack itself is phony and pretentious; for you to respond in kind is precisely correct. It will immediately tell your opponent that he or she is not dealing with a naive target but with someone who knows what's going on and is prepared to deal with it.

Let's look at one sample confrontation and then close this chapter with two practice sets for you to work on.

CONFRONTATION 20: *A HUSBAND & WIFE*

MARK: "*Some* husbands would really get up*set* if their wives insisted on going back to work when the kids were still only *babies*."

ANITA: "Really? It would be interesting to hear *your* opinion on the matter, darling."

MARK: *"My* opinion is that you have *no business* going back to work, if you really want to know!"

ANITA: "I see. Well, I'm willing to discuss that idea if you are."

Notice what has happened here. Mark, surprised and caught off guard, has abandoned all pretense of being some unique and superior individual to whom Anita should be grateful, and has switched from Computer Mode to Blaming. Now the issue is right out in the open, and Anita has made an offer to continue the discussion in Leveler Mode. This is properly done.

CONFRONTATION 21:
A FINANCIAL AID OFFICER (FAO) & A COLLEGE STUDENT

FAO CARTWRIGHT: "*Some* financial aid officers would be very unlikely to *believe* a student with a grade point average of only two-point-*six* and nothing but a flimsy explanation."

NEAL EVERETT: _____

_____

_____

_____

_____

_____

FAO: _____

_____

_____

_____

_____

_____

NEAL: _____

_____

_____

_____

_____

_____

FAO: _____

_____

_____

_____

_____

_____

NEAL: _____

_____

_____

_____

_____

_____

CONFRONTATION 22: *AN AUTO MECHANIC & A CUSTOMER*

BOB GRANGE: *"Some* skilled mechanics would consider it a real *in*sult if a customer came back and insinuated that work had been done on their car that wasn't really *ne*cessary."

SUE VERNER: _____

_____

_____

_____

BOB: _____

_____

_____

_____

_____

SUE: _____

_____

_____

_____

_____

BOB: _____

_____

_____

_____

_____

SUE: _____

_____

_____

_____

_____

SECTION H ATTACKS ON ME

DATE _____

SITUATION _____

_____

_____

_____

(FIRST MOVE) **WHAT MY OPPONENT SAID**

_____

_____

_____

WHAT I SAID

_____

_____

_____

WHAT I SHOULD HAVE SAID

_____

_____

_____

(SECOND MOVE) **WHAT MY OPPONENT SAID**

_____

_____

_____

WHAT I SAID

_____

_____

_____

WHAT I SHOULD HAVE SAID

(THIRD MOVE) WHAT MY OPPONENT SAID

WHAT I SAID

WHAT I SHOULD HAVE SAID

(FOURTH MOVE) WHAT MY OPPONENT SAID

WHAT I SAID

WHAT I SHOULD HAVE SAID

SAMPLE SCRIPTS

CONFRONTATION 21

FAO CARTWRIGHT: "*Some* financial aid officers would be very unlikely to *believe* a student with a grade point average of only two-point-*six* and nothing but a flimsy explanation."

NEAL EVERETT: "Really? It would be interesting to hear *your* opinion on the issue, Mr. Cartwright."

FAO: "*Doctor* Cartwright, Mr. Everett!"

NEAL: "Of course, Dr. Cartwright. My apologies."

FAO: "Now where were we, anyway?"

NEAL: "You were about to discuss the attitude of financial aid officers in situations of this kind, Dr. Cartwright. And I'm looking forward to that—this entire matter is a new area for me."

The student is doing this right—and it isn't easy to do it right. Among the other unpalatable facts of life is this one: there's no way to ask somebody to lend you money, or give you money, while at the same time maintaining an attitude of total independence. You don't have to give up your *dignity* in this situation. Begging is not required; spouting over-the-top compliments is not required. But anyone you are asking for money other than at gunpoint has more power than you have, and you need to keep that firmly in mind. There's a fine line between being appropriately respectful and being a toady; it's important to learn where that line is and how to walk it.

FAO Cartwright has given away a few points with his insistence on being called "Doctor" rather than "Mister," which probably means that the student's first move caught him off guard. Only if the FAO is insecure in his own estimate of his status would he demand the title in that way, instead of saying something more neutral, such as "I should mention that I'd rather be called Doctor Cartwright, Mr. Everett."

By the end of the set of moves in this sample script, Neal has the FAO in a position where it's going to be awkward to return to the original accusation, with all its dangling presuppositions. Who will win is difficult to predict, but things are going well for Neal. Just remember that if you're asking for money (or any substantial favor), it's very bad strategy to humiliate the person you're asking. On the other hand, money or favors that rob you of your self-respect have too high a price. Neal's closing line is just respectful enough.

FAO: *"Some* financial aid officers would be very unlikely to *believe* a student with a grade point average of only two-point-*six* and nothing but a flimsy explanation."

NEAL: "My story is *true*. And my grades are as good as *any*body's could be with the obligations I have to meet."

FAO: *"Mis*ter Everett—whining is *not* going to help matters. I sit here all day long and listen to whiners, and I get very tired of it."

NEAL: "Then maybe you're in the wrong job, Mr. Cartwright."

FAO: "And maybe you are in the wrong *school,* Mr. Everett."

NEAL: "Okay, okay . . . I get it."

This student gets the message, but not the loan; and it took him about three minutes to lose it. He now has the satisfaction of his intact pride, but he has no money to pay for his tuition, and he has also given the FAO a chance to dump additional abuse on him for free. This is *not* cost-effective. If Neal is going to be turned down for the money anyway, he might at least come out of the verbal confrontation with a few more points earned.

FAO: *"Some* financial aid officers would be very unlikely to *believe* a student with a grade point average of only two-point-*six* and nothing but a flimsy explanation."

NEAL: "I've heard people say that a lot, and it's an interesting idea."

FAO: "You spend a lot of time applying for loans, do you?"

NEAL: "Sorry—I don't think I follow you."

FAO: "Well, young man, unless your circle of friends includes numerous financial aid officers, bank loan officers, and the like—which I sincerely doubt—I don't know where you would have heard people discussing the appropriate attitude for officials in charge of disbursements of monies to dubious applicants."

NEAL: "Sorry, sir. I guess I was out of line."

This is the sort of thing that you risk when you tinker with a response to a Section H attack. Neal's mistake was in not going to Computer Mode: he begins with personal language ("I've heard people say that") and leaves himself wide open for FAO to knock around. Neal's mistake has cost him, whether he gets the loan or not. He ends up having to apologize and behave like a doormat. Not recommended. On the other hand, his apology is both neutral and appropriate, and is the proper move.

FAO: *"Some* financial aid officers would be very unlikely to *believe* a student with a grade point average of only two-point-*six* and nothing but a flimsy explanation."

NEAL: "One hears that said a good deal. It would be most interesting to hear *your* opinion on the matter, Dr. Cartwright."

FAO: "One does, does one?"

NEAL: "I'm sorry?"

FAO: "Another thing one hears—if one listens to the right people—is that when you're asking someone for money you don't start by proving that you could qualify for an Olympic medal in arrogance."

NEAL: "Yes, sir."

Again, Neal has tried to make a few small changes. And it's quite true that using the indefinite "one" in his response takes him out of the sentence and puts it in Computer Mode. Unfortunately, by using this construction Neal has escalated the pompousness of the dialogue and outpompoused the FAO. This is very risky. Most powerful people, if they have any goodwill in their character, have reservations about picking on people who aren't remotely their equals in status. But Neal has canceled that out. His response says, "Look, you pompous creep, you don't need to use kid gloves on *me*." Once he delivers that message, FAO Cartwright is no longer bound by any code of not kicking underdogs; on the contrary, Neal has released him from that and demanded to be treated as an equal. He has only himself to thank when he gets precisely what he asked for. FAO Cartwright is playing the game by the rules, and Neal is going to lose.

Be absolutely certain before you declare yourself ready to play verbal games with no holds barred that you really *are* ready.

Or that you can afford to look upon being verbally thrashed as an educational experience.

CONFRONTATION 22

BOB GRANGE: *"Some* skilled mechanics would consider it a real *in*sult if a customer came back and insinuated that work had been done on their car that wasn't really *ne*cessary."

SUE VERNER: "Really? It would be interesting to hear *your* opinion on the matter, Mr. Grainger."

BOB: "You just heard it."

SUE: "I don't think I followed you."

BOB: "You want me to spell it out for you?"

SUE: "That would be an excellent idea."

This is going properly. Bob is now going to have to be absolutely specific, which will give Sue a chance to deal with the situation as a Leveler. And Bob has abandoned his abstract Computer stance without a struggle. Sue is ahead.

BOB GRANGE: *"Some* skilled mechanics would consider it a real *in*sult if a customer came back and insinuated that work had been done on their car that wasn't really *ne*cessary."

SUE VERNER: "That's interesting."

BOB: "Interesting? What do you mean by *that*?"

SUE: "You read about mechanics who—in spite of their skill—are touchy and defensive about any attempt at a logical adult discussion of their bills . . . and you can't help wondering why that should be so. After all, the mechanic is the expert, not the customer, right?"

BOB: "Absolutely."

SUE: "What do you suppose accounts for this problem, Mr. Grange—speaking as a skilled mechanic yourself?"

Sue is ahead, and it will be interesting to see what the mechanic does next. He can move to an abstract discussion of other mechanics and other estimates, losing money as he whiles away time with this pleasant customer who is so interested in all his opinions. Or he can change his strategy and try Leveling. Or he can try to think of something else. He of course knows that Sue is putting him on, but he started this himself and will have to get out of it the same way.

BOB GRANGE: "*Some* skilled mechanics would consider it a real *in*sult if a customer came back and insinuated that work had been done on their car that wasn't really *n*ecessary."

SUE VERNER: "Too bad you aren't a skilled mechanic, then, isn't it?"

BOB: "You want to see my credentials? I'll be only too happy to show them to you. Or maybe you'd like to talk to the service manager."

SUE: "Listen, *n*obody talks to *me* like that!"

BOB: "One more time . . . let's go see the service manager."

SUE: "The only person I plan on seeing is my *law*yer, and believe me, I'm going to have a *lot* to say to *her*!"

Even if Sue does go to court, does win the lawsuit, and does get the car repaired properly at a proper price, the mechanic has won this confrontation. She has done everything wrong, and even if it's true that this mechanic has tried to charge for unnecessary repairs, it's Sue who will be without a car while the repairs are being done. It's also Sue who will have to spend time in court instead of going to work or to school or taking the kids to the beach. The fact that Bob is also being inconvenienced won't cancel out all that time and money and effort wasted. (His next line, by the way, would have been "Suit yourself!")

BOB GRANGE: "*Some* skilled mechanics would consider it a real *in*sult if a customer came back and insinuated that work had been done on their car that wasn't really *necessary*."

SUE VERNER: "How nice to know that you're not one of those, Mr. Grange."

BOB: "Oh, I see. You're not going to play that game."

SUE: "No. I'm not. Now let's take another look at that bill, please."

This is expertly done—and risky. Sue should try this only if she knows the work of an auto mechanic upside down and backwards and is prepared to prove it. If you happen to be in that fortunate position, you can afford to try this. A Leveling challenge with a mechanic, a carpenter, or a skilled craftsman of any kind is appropriate—and safe—only if your skills are at the same level. Otherwise, some other strategy should be chosen.

12

SUPPLEMENTARY TECHNIQUE 1:
Body Language

Up to now, much of this book has been written as though it were possible and logical to separate the words that are spoken from the rest of their delivery. I've used this artificial separation for two purposes: to let us look at surface patterns that occur in utterances and to simplify the process of relating those surface patterns to the unspoken presuppositions that lie behind them.

This has been useful and convenient, but it can't go on forever, since in real life we don't carry on conversations that are made up only of words. For any utterance, there will be at least two active communication channels: ① the verbal channel represented by the words themselves; and ② a *nonverbal* channel that goes along with the words, at the same time, which must be considered just as thoroughly in verbal self-defense. (The fact that this underlying nonverbal channel would ideally include the entire real world doesn't make life—or this book—any simpler.)

Much research indicates that when the verbal channel and the nonverbal channel are in conflict and you have no solid information to tell you which one is reliable, the right strategy is to believe the nonverbal message. An example of verbal/nonverbal channel conflict, first pointed out to me by John Grinder, and which I have seen many times since then, is the person who says "I love them so much, there's *nothing* I wouldn't do for them!" while at the same time pounding his fist on the nearest surface and slowly turning his head from side to side. In such a case, unless you have special clarifying information to the contrary, your best strategy is to assume that in fact the man does *not* love the persons in question.

The nonverbal channel is made up of so many different things that its study has spawned a large set of technical terms in communication fields and in linguistics. You will read of *kinesics, proxemics, pragmatics, paralinguistics, haptics,* and more. None of these terms is exactly right for this chapter; but then, the term I've chosen—*body language*—isn't exactly right, either. I selected it because it's a familiar term and it does cover in a rough way what will be discussed here. However, as used in the popular and mass media it typically refers only to gestures, posture, and facial expression; I will be using it more broadly than that.

Let's understand it to mean the fullest extension of the phrase "the language of the body," the entire nonverbal channel as it is used in language interactions. It will then include, for the purposes of this book, not only gestures, posture, and facial expressions, but many other things as well. For example, it will include the quality and tone of the voice, the intonation (the tune the words are set to), the physical distance between speaker(s) and listener(s), the messages conveyed by the way a speaker chooses to clothe and/or decorate the body, the method a speaker uses to decide when it is his or her turn to talk, and so on.

Because doing this topic justice would require an entire separate book, I am going to concentrate my attention on three specific areas of body language that are both useful in verbal self-defense and suitable for novices. (You'll find suggested readings at the end of this book to lead you into more advanced material if you want to explore further.) First I want to discuss the proper use of the voice itself as an *instrument* for producing words, just as you would talk of the proper use of a musical instrument to produce a melody. Next I want to take up very briefly the proper arrangement of the parts of the body, and their best positioning in relation to the physical setting and other person(s) involved in the language interaction. Finally, I want to talk about *mannerisms*, language habits that may be deliberate or that a speaker may not be aware of. In terms of techniques that can be quickly learned for maximum positive effect, these three areas are the most promising.

PROPER USE OF THE VOICE

Voice "quality" is a mysterious thing. It involves pitch and nasality and volume and breathiness and harshness and timbre ("timbre" being that even more mysterious quality that tells you whether the instrument you hear being played is a violin or a flute or a piano), and more. Experts called "phoneticians" can tell you more than you'll ever want to know about all of these things, but learning to control each one of them consciously and blend all those separate controls into a natural whole is impossible. Fortunately, it needn't be possible. You don't have to know consciously what adjustments to make in your muscles and nerves and joints in order to walk. Like the centipede that was doing fine until somebody told her that she had one hundred separate legs to manage, an attempt at such conscious knowledge would only make you fail. You make all the necessary adjustments without "knowing" what you're doing, and your body has the same skill available for using the voice as it does for using the legs and feet.

This is fortunate, because—although it is utterly unfair to do so—people judge other people on the basis of their voice quality, often without taking anything else into account. If others perceive your voice as "whiny" (perhaps because it's high and nasal and thin), your utterances are going to be perceived that way, too, and that affects others' perception of your personality. If your voice is perceived as gruff and harsh, you are likely to be considered cross and bullying; if it's breathless and badly controlled, people will assume that you are slightly feather-headed and untrustworthy.

The reason that how you say something is often more important than the words you say is that in English a very large portion of the *emotional* message that goes with your words is carried by the body language. I can say the words "You're an absolute saint" in such a way that you clearly understand that I despise you; I can say the words "You're an absolute monster" in such a way that the emotional message you hear is "I love you with all my heart." In English the *way* you talk can interfere with, or even cancel, your actual words.

Things *should not be this way*. People should not automatically label others on the basis of voice quality, any more than they should judge them on the basis of such things as haircut or accent or clothing. People should be able to rely on the words they say being understood on the basis of their meanings in the dictionary, without being undercut by body language. Subjective judgments should have no effect on the words being said or the impression listeners have of the kind of person saying them. But as Robert Day said in a brilliant *New Yorker* cartoon in 1970, we are in the real world, where we cannot change the channel.

You, as a student of verbal self-defense, can make a real effort not to judge people by the characteristics of their voices. You can do your best to withhold your judgment of others until you have some better information to base it on than the way their voices sound to you. But you cannot safely assume, ever, that other people will pay you that same courtesy. Therefore, knowing how your voice sounds to others is a crucial part of your self-defense skills, and a pleasant voice quality is crucially important to your success in this world. It would not be an overstatement to say that getting rid of an *unpleasant* voice quality is even more important, simply because that quality can in fact weaken or even invalidate all the rest of your communication skills.

Similarly, if it seems to you that there is a large gap between the words you're hearing and the emotional message that you're getting, you can try not to leap to conclusions. You can listen to the other person for a long enough period of time to become absolutely certain that you're not misunderstanding.

Improving Your Own Voice

Begin by making a recording of your voice, in ordinary conversation with a friend, using an ordinary cassette recorder or similar device, and then listening to it carefully. What you want to find out is how you sound under typical conditions, not in a recording studio. Your recording should be at least half an hour long, to give you and your friend a chance to get over feeling self-conscious about being recorded and start speaking naturally.

My personal experience is that when people who aren't used to listening to their recorded voices hear themselves speaking, they immediately declare that that is *not* how they sound. Some of this is a technical matter, but for the most part the problem is that the voice they hear doesn't match their personal image of the way they sound. Since it's possible that the recording could be defective in some way, if you have this reaction by all means get a second opinion. Ask someone who's accustomed to hearing you talk whether the recording sounds like you to them or not. Unless there really is a mechanical problem, ninety-nine out of one hundred times what you are hearing *is* the way you sound to other people—which is what you're trying to find out. Knowing that you sound like Diane Sawyer or Wolf Blitzer to your *self* is a useless piece of information unless other people share that perception, and if they don't share it it's a dangerous illusion that you need to give up immediately. If you are convinced that you sound like Sawyer or Blitzer but other people hear you as someone with a high squeaky voice, one of your major communication problems has been identified.

Suppose you discover that your voice quality is unpleasant. Then what? Rarely, that unpleasantness will be an actual speech disability requiring the attention of a medical expert or a speech therapist. If that's your situation, try to get the expert help you need, because it will be worth every penny. People tend to quickly forget minor physical differences from the norm; once they've noticed that you have what they perceive as, say, an unusually big nose, they get used to it and disregard it. Your voice, however, doesn't share that "fading perception" advantage. Instead, the more you talk, the more aware people become of whatever it is that they find unpleasant about your voice, and the greater a barrier it is to your success in communication. This is a serious problem.

Let's assume (as will ordinarily be true) that the problem isn't a genuine disability. In that case, I am happy to be able to tell you that there's something you can do about it, that you can do it at your own convenience and without hiring any sort of expert, and that you can begin working on it at once. Here are the steps for you to follow.

① Get it straight in your own mind that your goal is to sound like *yourself,* but with a pleasant voice quality. I warn you about this because the technique I'm about to describe would indeed let you train yourself to sound like Diane Sawyer or Wolf Blitzer, and that would be a mistake. It would only make people consider you some kind of flake who thinks impersonations are appropriate for ordinary conversation.

② Buy or borrow or rent a device for making your recording, plus whatever other items would be needed for five or six hours of operation.

③ Find a friend whose voice quality *you* perceive as pleasant, who is of your gender and generation and ethnic heritage, and who is willing to help you out. Have your friend make at least two twenty-minute recordings for you, in ordinary speech—which does not mean reading aloud or reciting something memorized. Ask your friend to talk about "The Teacher I Hated Most When I Was a Kid" and "Why I Do/ Don't Like the President" and "My Most Embarrassing Experience" and "What I Like To Eat" and so on. Ordinary talking-to-somebody-else talking.

[*Note: If it's genuinely impossible for you to do this, you can substitute recordings of some public figure who has the sort of speech quality you want for yourself and who also meets the necessary specifications for age and gender and ethnicity. But a friend is the better choice, because the friend will be providing you with natural speech as your model instead of "performance" speech.]* You will work with your recordings in privacy and at your own convenience. How fast you do this is up to you, but it has to be done correctly.

④ Do *not* listen to a sentence on the recording, stop the recording, repeat the sentence, and then do that over and over again. That will only train you in your present vocal habits even more thoroughly than you were trained before. Instead, pick any sentence you want to work with, listen to it several times, and try to say that sentence *along with the speaker on the recording*. Do that over and over again until you can do it easily; then choose a new sentence and repeat the process. Be sure that you don't write down the sentence and read it back with the speaker; that won't produce natural speech.

Why does this work? Because as you try to speak along with the recorded sound you will, below the level of your conscious awareness, notice tiny differences between your own speech and the speech you're using as a model. Differences of volume, pitch, timbre, and so on. You will then try to *reduce* those differences, making use of the constant feedback between the two streams of sound, with your brain saying, "Now that's closer on the pitch, but let's turn the volume down a bit ... yeah, that's better, but now there's too much nasal there, let's cut that back . . . better, but there's still a difference ... let's see, how about putting the volume back *up* a tad ... yeah ..." and so on.

You can't do this consciously. Nobody can. And I'm not suggesting that there is any real physical level at which your brain is actually running through that monologue; it's just a way of explaining what's happening without going into a lecture on neurolinguistics, psychoacoustics, the anatomy and psychology of perception, and the like. Below the level of your conscious awareness, if you trust yourself and let the mechanisms of your body and mind take over the job, you *can* do this. You will gradually reduce the differences between the recording and your own speech, a little at a time, until they are a good match. (And if you go on fiendishly at this, you can keep it up until they're a *perfect* match. At which point you will have trained yourself to sound like you're trying to impersonate your friend. Remember, this is not your goal.)

⑤ Every two weeks, make a new recording of yourself talking for about five minutes, and listen to it. When your voice quality begins to sound pleasant, *stop*. You have gone far enough. If you're not sure you can trust your judgment and think you may just have gotten accustomed to the way you sound, get a second opinion again. Chances are that you have indeed fixed your problem. From then on, you need only check once in a while to be sure you haven't gone back to your old vocal habits.

Emphatic Stress On Words And Parts Of Words

Before we leave this subject, I want to take up briefly the topic of emphatic acoustic stress—often called just "emphasis." This has been mentioned before; for instance, when I've pointed out that the difference between a verbal attack and a Leveler's neutral utterance is often signaled only by the presence or absence of stress on a word such as "really." But stress is so very important in English, where it actually changes the meaning of what you're saying, that I think a bit more explanation and discussion would be helpful. The classic example type from linguistics, used by everyone but first pointed out by Edward Klima, goes like this:

① **"What are we having for dinner, Daddy?"**

② **"What are we having for dinner—*Daddy*?"**

Sentence 1 asks Daddy what the dinner menu will be; Sentence 2 asks somebody else whether Daddy is going to be the main course. That's a big difference in meaning to be riding on stress and rhythm alone, but English works that way. In fact, one of the quickest ways a native speaker of another language can spot native American English speakers is by their frequent tendency to use English emphatic stress in every other language they learn, whether the other language has that characteristic or not. European French, for example, doesn't have it, but Americans rarely let that stand in their way when they're speaking French. Emphatic stress is heard as either higher pitch or greater volume or both. It has to be handled with great care, since its function is to call attention to some part of the utterance, and since it always brings with it presuppositions that may or may not be reflected on the surface. Look at the following set of sentences, with their meanings spelled out for clarity:

① **A.** "John is the only man in the room." [Neutral statement of fact, meaning "This room contains only one male human being, the individual named John."]

② **B.** "*John* is the only man in the room." ["John—not the other person or persons I just heard mentioned—is, in my opinion, the only male human being in the room."]

③ **C.** "John *is* the only man in the room." ["John—despite the statement made by another person or persons to the contrary, is, in my opinion, the only male human being in the room."]

④ **D.** "John is the only man in the *room*." ["There may be male human beings in the car or in the basement or somewhere else, but in my opinion the only male human being actually in the room itself is John, and I want you to be aware that it is my opinion, because I consider it important."]

We could go on with more such examples, but these four are enough to demonstrate the power, and the danger, of English stress. Whenever you hear emphatic stresses in an utterance, take that as a signal to listen carefully. And then expand that utterance into everything you can tell it means, as I did in the examples above. If you don't have time to do this in conversations, try to jot down the sentence to analyze later. With practice you'll learn to do this as rapidly as any other kind of verbal processing, and it will be on automatic. And remember to give the same care and attention to your *own* use of stress. It matters.

You will notice that the stresses in sequences of hostile language don't always appear in exactly the same places. You may hear "If you *really* loved me" on one occasion and "If you really *loved* me" on another, for example. There are complicated rules that control the placement of these stresses, but you don't need to worry about them. If you are a native speaker of English, your internal mental grammar will always tell you where the stresses belong and how to interpret them.

Finally, it's important to give people who aren't native or fluent speakers of English the benefit of the doubt when you hear them use emphatic stresses, as well as when they hear you use them and don't seem to understand what you're saying. Someone whose native language is Spanish or Farsi or Chinese may say "Even *you* should be able to solve this problem" without being aware that it's insulting. Similarly, they may not understand the emotional messages that go with the emphatic stresses you use in sentences you say to them.

PROPER PLACEMENT OF THE BODY

One of the biggest dangers for the beginner in verbal self-defense is the oversimplification of body language that has found its way into so much of the popular media. This is probably an unavoidable problem; writing about any technical subject for a general audience almost requires oversimplification. But information that can only be understood if you already have an advanced degree in the field is no use to the beginner, and refusing to try to make things clear for fear of being called a "popularizer" is a position that tends to make ignorance of the subject a permanent and widespread condition.

All that I can do here is caution you not to take for granted the accuracy of everything you read about body language. The idea that a particular set of gestures, a particular way of crossing the feet or legs, a particular way of wrinkling the forehead, can be relied on always to have the same meaning in every person you encounter is a myth. People who write books on the subject rarely mean to give readers that impression and can usually be counted on to tell you that they're talking about most of the people, most of the time, in a specific cultural or ethnic group. But magazine articles, quick spots on television or radio programs, newspaper stories and brief reviews with quotes taken out of context, as well as speeches by instant experts, all tend to ignore these warnings. You get the idea that you can memorize a list of gestures, facial expressions, and postures along with a list of their "meanings" and then rely on that universally. This is totally false. You can't even rely on such a list for *one* person in a single culture all of the time. A gesture that means one thing in your own dialect may mean a number of different things to other ethnic groups and/or other generations. Do your best never to use a nonverbal item cross-culturally without checking it out carefully first, to the extent that such things are under your control.

One of the major reasons why Computer Mode is the safest stance for beginners in verbal self-defense is that it's the mode with the fewest gestures, the least variation in facial expression, and the most neutral intonation and tone of voice. That doesn't mean it has no dangers at all on the nonverbal channel, but it's the least dangerous of the Satir Modes you can choose.

Be sensitive to personal distance—to the size of the personal space that other people want to have around them. It varies from one group to another. Much research shows that Hispanics need a smaller personal space than do Anglos, which leads to language interactions during which the Hispanic keeps trying to move closer as the Anglo keeps trying to move farther away, and the end result is an Anglo with back to the wall because he or she cannot back up any farther.

Since you can't possibly know what the favored personal space of every individual you talk to will be, you need a general technique to help you in every situation—a rough rule of thumb. It goes like this: When the person you're talking to keeps moving closer to you, making you feel a little crowded, assume that that person needs a smaller personal space than you do for conversation, and *hold still*. If he or she then stops moving in on you, you're made the right decision, and things will go better, provided that you can handle your own feeling of being hemmed in. Conversely, if the person you're talking to keeps backing up, assume that he or she needs a bigger personal space than you require, and stop trying to get closer. If you're right, again, things will improve. In both cases, the remedy is to hold still and let the other person set the limits of the conversational space. Remember what you did, remember how it worked (or didn't work), and add it to your records. Don't assume that it will always work for another person of that particular ethnic group, age group, and gender, but make a note that will help you spot rough general patterns for late use.

Finally, be aware that the way you dress, and where and how you place your body, make up a large part of the meaning in any verbal interaction. You have every right to go to a job interview for a junior executive position with a stuffy Fortune 500 corporation wearing your hair loose down your back, a full beard, or no bra (whichever of these fits your situation), and flip flops. That is your moral right, and nobody is entitled to take it away from you. Similarly, you have the right to sit slouched in your chair through that interview, staring at the ceiling, if you want to. But it is foolish to be unaware that by making the decision to do those things you are delivering a lengthy message. It runs something like this, on the nonverbal channel:

> **"Okay, here I am. I know what a junior executive around here is supposed to look like, but I don't happen to give a damn about that. This is how I look, this is the way I prefer to look, and whether you like the way I look doesn't interest me. If you want to hire me, you hire me like this, because this is how I am, and you might just as well know it right from the start."**

You may be so good, so highly skilled, that that message won't keep you from being hired. The person interviewing you may be overwhelmed by your rugged individualism, your honesty, your courage, your outstanding resume, or some combination of all these things. But be *aware* that you are saying all of that even if every overt word you say is in a nice polite "Yes, sir/No, sir" style, and that the full message is sure to be heard.

If you don't care to deliver that message, you'd be well advised to do a little research before you go into a verbal interaction. Find out what your audience usually looks like by looking at some people who are part of it and observing what they ordinarily wear and how they ordinarily take up a position in conversation. Let that be your guide, to whatever degree you are willing to make such adjustments.

MANNERISMS

A mannerism, in the context of this book, is a language habit. A striking and obvious example of a mannerism is the use of multiple emphatic stresses in a single utterance, like this:

> **"If you *really* mean what you *say* about student *rights*, then you *won't make* us write *term* papers if we don't *want* to."**

"While *I* was walking *over* here I saw a *woman* walking three *huge* dogs and just one *tiny little white* dog, and I wondered how on *earth* she could manage *all that* at *once.*"

For people to use stress this way is as irritating as if they continually hummed under their breath or cracked their knuckles. It's typical only of small children ["*Mom*my, I *saw* a *snow*man and it *had* a *carrot* for a *nose!*"] and of adults who don't mind sounding like small children. This kind of stress is intended, you'll recall, to focus attention on a particular part of an utterance; when it turns up in half a dozen different places, it becomes impossible to tell what matters to the speaker. It takes only a sentence or two of this kind to provoke either anger or an end to any pretense of listening. Emphatic stress should be used sparingly.

Another example is the gesture many teachers have, at all levels—shaking their index finger at someone while they're talking, with the rest of the hand in a tight fist. Teachers may start out doing this only deliberately, but by the time they've taught for ten years it frequently becomes a habit they're no longer aware of. It's a threatening gesture, and a hostile one. A standard progression is for a new teacher to use the gesture to convince a child that he or she is *not* going to be allowed to hit other students with the wooden blocks—and that's appropriate. Ten years later that same teacher, talking to a close friend about almost any subject, is shaking that finger nonstop—and that is *not* appropriate. In teachers of retirement age it may become something they do even when they're talking on the phone, which is hilarious. When I taught teachers, I told them that this particular mannerism is so dangerously habit-forming that they needed to decide at the very beginning never to use it—even if it means that at first they have to clasp their hands behind their backs to keep from using it. Of the two mannerisms, the one with hands behind the back is by far the lesser of two evils.

To break yourself of *any* mannerism, by the way, this is the rule of thumb: Choose some neutral Computer Mode posture that doesn't allow you to do whatever the mannerism requires, and use that to break yourself of the bad habit. Try not to acquire the Computer Mode posture as a new mannerism; this is an obvious danger. Nevertheless, I will defend to the last fall the proposition that if you must have bad nonverbal habits, the Computer Mode ones are the best bad ones to have.

As was true for judging personal space requirements with little information, you can handle unwanted mannerisms by paying careful attention; by writing down and analyzing what you observe, in order to record general patterns; and by letting the other person determine the limits so far as is possible. If someone is shaking his or her finger at you constantly in that Teacher Gesture, assume that it's a mannerism and cancel your automatic "Hey, I'm being threatened!" response. Don't respond with threatening stuff of your own. If *you* are doing the finger shaking and the other person is reacting negatively, have sense and skill enough to realize what's happening and stop.

If you don't know what it is about your nonverbal behavior that's causing the trouble, but you notice that the atmosphere is heating up, try assuming full Computer Mode stance and maintaining that until you have more information.

[A word of warning: you'll find books and articles that tell you to work with this and other problems of nonverbal communication by matching your own body language to that of the person you're dealing with. This is an extremely powerful technique, and it can be learned, but it's for experts only. If you fumble it—for example, if you cause the other person to think that you are mocking him or her—you'll be in trouble. Not recommended.]

The major characteristics of the Computer Mode nonverbal channel, for most native speakers of English, will be these:

1. Very few gestures, or none at all

2. Very little facial expression—the minimum that can be used without giving the impression that you're not listening

3. Very little *change* in body language. That is, whatever position and expression the Computer starts out with is maintained almost without alteration through the whole interaction

4. No sudden movements or abrupt changes of expression or posture; everything is done calmly and without surface evidence of emotion

5. Neutral intonation and tone of voice, with very few emphatic stresses on words and parts of words

6. No body language that's typical of the other Satir Modes. No Blamer body language such as pounding fists or shouting; no Placater body language such as whining or crying or wringing the hands; no Distracter body language such as constantly fooling with hair or glasses, or some mixture of other Satir Mode nonverbal behaviors

Avoid mannerisms that represent an "in" joke, if you can. For example, a gesture that marks you as an amateur in a job interview—thus costing you points—is the one where you reach up with one hand and take off your glasses by the earpiece, hold the glasses in the area around your chin, and stare intently into the interviewer's eyes as you say something. The more you do this, the funnier it will become to the interviewer, who will perceive that as evidence that you don't know what you're doing. *Watch* the person you're talking with. If he or she reacts to some item of your body language with what looks like a struggle not to laugh, give that item up at once. (An expert interviewer shouldn't be this transparent, but it does turn out that way sometimes.)

Avoid interpreting another person's body language in terms of unquestioned Popular Wisdom. For instance, most native speakers of mainstream American English have been brought up to believe something roughly like this: "All people who won't look you in the eye are dishonest." There are ethnic groups for whom the Popular Wisdom is "All people who insist on looking you in the eye are rude." When one person is avoiding direct eye contact to keep from being thought rude, and the other person assumes that this is evidence of dishonesty, communication is going to break down, and the consequences may be unfortunate.

What makes this dangerous rather than trivial is that usually neither of the persons involved is aware of what's happening. The interviewer turns you down or doesn't hire you on the basis of "a gut feeling that you just aren't the right person for the job." You decide that this happened because the interviewer is prejudiced against your ethnic group, gender, age, lifestyle, or whatever is *your* most common "gut feeling" about these things. You're both wrong, the interaction was a failure, and the whole process has just been reinforced in both of you in such a way that it will go on happening.

Whichever side of the interaction you are on, your guiding principle should be: *pay attention and don't leap to conclusions.* Give the other person the benefit of the doubt until you have information to work with.

This chapter is already a long and heavy one, and it's time to wind it up. I want to close by tackling the idea that all these things are somehow a massive compromise of your principles. In my workshops and seminars, people sometimes say that they refuse to "suck up" to other people or to "talk down" to other people, in these ways. This is a serious misunderstanding, and it needs to be straightened out.

In verbal self-defense, as in any of the physical martial arts, the ideal—the undoubtedly unattainable ideal—is never to have to use what you know, because you're able to head off all confrontations before they start and only Leveling takes place. Not because you are a gutless wonder but because you know what you're doing. A major factor in working toward that goal is the ability to *reduce tension* in any kind of verbal interaction. All of the information I've been discussing in this chapter is for that purpose—for lowering the level of tension and emotion in verbal encounters so that a move to Leveling becomes possible. These actions aren't techniques for verbal self-debasement; they are *defusing* techniques. They require great skill and carry with them great honor.

13

SUPPLEMENTARY TECHNIQUE 2:

Being Charismatic

"Charisma" is a mysterious word. People are said to "have" it in the same way that they "have" brown eyes. Charisma is viewed as something you are born with, a gift from the Fates, and something as inseparably a part of you as your eyes and your heart. Definitions of charisma (except for the one specifically from Christian theology) are not very illuminating. A fair summary would go something like this: charisma is a mysterious, irresistible, almost magical ability to make others believe what you say to them and be willing, even eager, to do what you ask of them.

If people believe you because of the logic of what you say, the cause is not your charisma. There is a very substantial body of research indicating that logic is almost useless as a tool for convincing and persuading people. If people do what you ask them to do simply because you have the power to force them to—with a gun or a whip or a spanking or a failing grade or a three-week assignment to latrine duty—the cause is not your charisma. The crucial difference between coercion and charisma is that we *want* to believe the charismatic individual, we want to do whatever he or she asks of us, and we don't care about other factors. It's said that Adlai Stevenson, when complimented on a speech, once pointed out that people often told him what nice speeches he gave, but that after John F. Kennedy's speeches they said, "Let's march!" *That* is charisma.

Charisma is a matter of perception. In the discussion of English emphatic stress in Chapter Twelve, I told you that it's heard as higher pitch and louder volume; experts in acoustics and phonetics would tell you that that's a mighty inadequate description. For the purposes of verbal self-defense, however, it's that perception that is crucial; that perception triggers the responses in the listener that make stress so tricky and so useful. Charisma, too, whatever its scientific explanation might be, is *perceived*—seen and heard and felt—as the ability to convince and compel without force. And it's that perception that concerns us here. The interesting question is: can you learn to bring about that perception in people who are listening to you? I believe you can.

Nobody has ever developed a test to measure someone's Charisma Quotient, so far as I know. But if we had one, everything you have learned from this book so far would raise your CQ score a little bit, and the information yet to come will continue that process. Just how high you can go on the charisma scale will depend on many things, some of which are indeed a matter of the Fates. No question about it, it helps a lot to be physically attractive, in glorious health, and wealthy. The one thing that matters most, however, is how hard you are willing to work at it.

A warning: don't confuse charisma with Leveling. The man trapped in a stalled elevator, feeling scared, looking scared, and saying he's scared, is Leveling; whether he's also charismatic is something you can't know unless you are there to judge. Similarly, the woman who knows the car she's trying to sell you is a bad buy, but who successfully uses both her verbal and nonverbal communication channels to convince you that you should be delighted to buy it, is clearly charismatic, but she is not Leveling. In the chapter on emergency techniques we'll take on the problem of how to spot and deal with that most dangerous of communicating humans, the *phony* Leveler. In this chapter we are going to look at several techniques for being charismatic that are simple to learn and that will give you a good return on your investment of time and effort.

PREFERRED SENSORY MODES

Researchers over the years, especially in the field of education, have noted that people seem to have individual preferences for the use of one kind of sensory information over other kinds. This research has concentrated most heavily on vision and hearing, although recently a bit more attention has been paid to touch, taste, and smell. To my knowledge, John Grinder and Richard Bandler were the first to publish work on how people demonstrate these preferences specifically in their *language* behavior. I'm going to focus here on one aspect of this subject that can be a useful addition to your set of verbal self-defense techniques.

If we assume that it's usual for people to prefer one of their sensory systems and agree that they will often make their preference clear in their language, we can set up a list of examples, like this:

SIGHT
- "I see what you mean."
- "That's very clear."
- "That looks good to me."

HEARING

- "I hear what you're trying to say."
- "What you're saying is just a lot of noise to me."
- "That sounds fine to me."

TOUCH

- "Somehow, this situation rubs me the wrong way."
- "I can't put my finger on the problem, but I just don't get it."
- "That feels okay to me."

SMELL

- "This is a really fishy situation, if you ask me."
- "I'll sniff around and find out what's going on."
- "That smells rotten to me."

TASTE

- "This whole thing leaves a bad taste in my mouth."
- "This is a sweet deal."
- "That really makes me sick at my stomach."

Language that uses the sensory systems of smell and taste seems to be more rare than language reflecting sight, hearing, and touch. (Smell and taste are often treated as a single system, because they are so closely connected.) This may be because so few people develop these senses to any extent—exceptions would include perfume specialists and wine tasters—or it may be due to a shortage of English vocabulary items for expressing smell and taste perceptions, or both. Or there may be a quite different explanation. It would take much more research to settle this question.

For our purposes here, what's important is the technique of matching the *sensory mode*—the *vocabulary* of a particular sensory system—that the person you're talking with is using. Look at these two brief exchanges:

X: "That's my proposal. Now I'd like to know if it's clear and if you see any problems with it."

Y: "No, it really looks good to me."

[Sensory modes match.]

X: "That's my proposal. Now I'd like to know if it's clear and if you see any problems with it."

Y: "No, it really sounds good to me."

[Sensory modes clash.]

Although both of B's responses "mean" the same thing, in the sense that both express approval of A's proposal, they differ in that one uses the technique of sensory mode matching and the other does not. This isn't trivial, particularly in a communication situation where a confrontational atmosphere can be predicted in advance, such as a meeting between labor and management, or a courtroom trial. Often you can use the sensory mode matching technique unobtrusively as a way of keeping the level of tension in a discussion lower than it might otherwise be, and the minor effort required is well worth the result. Look at the following example.

CONFRONTATION 23: *A TEACHER & STUDENT*

TEACHER: "Look, Billy, your problem in school is no mystery. It's obvious—*any*body can see that you just don't try."

BILLY: "I *do* try! I work on it all the time! I just don't *get* it, that's all!"

TEACHER: "Billy . . . come on now. Your spelling, for instance. Do you really expect me to believe that you study those words the way you're supposed to, and still miss almost every one of them on your tests? I'm not blind, you know, *or* stupid."

BILLY: "And I guess that means I'm both. And a liar, too."

TEACHER: "I didn't say that."

BILLY: "Well, that's how what you're saying makes me feel."

TEACHER: "Billy, you *have* to try not to see everything I do to help you as a personal attack. That's a very murky way of looking at things."

BILLY: "Now I'm crazy, too. Thanks a lot!"

TEACHER: "You see? With that attitude, there's no way anybody can help you!"

BILLY: "Okay, okay! I'm sorry. I give up!"

TEACHER: "As I said—it's not that you can't do the work, it's that you *won't* do it. That's very clear. I hope you see the difference."

This teacher, who has used sight vocabulary again and again, while the student has relied on touch vocabulary, now has a totally hostile and alienated youngster to deal with. Billy is of course now convinced that Teacher has no respect for him at all and cares nothing about him—which may or may not be true.

We would be far beyond oversimplification if I were to claim that sensory mode matching is a cure for every problem, or that it would automatically eliminate the difficulties between Billy and the teacher. Done properly, however, sensory mode matching is a powerful way to reduce potential conflict and build trust and rapport. It makes your listener feel that the two of you are "on the same wavelength" and "speak the same language," that you are an understanding and empathic person, and that you are a pleasure to talk to. In short, it makes you more charismatic.

Learning to do this quickly and naturally takes practice. You should add it to your journal work, because you will need to do some advance practice to prepare for real-life situations. First, find out what your own preferred sensory mode is, by paying attention to the language you yourself use. (If you find it hard to decide, ask some of your family or close friends to help you.) Then practice identifying other people's preferred sensory modes by paying attention to *their* language behavior patterns. Finally, practice translating utterances from one sensory mode to another.

To do this, you'll need to be aware of *predicates*, because that's where many of your clues will come from. English has four kinds of predicates, as in the example sentences below, where the predicate is everything to the right of the pound sign in the sentence.

ENGLISH PREDICATES—EXAMPLES

True verbs: Tracy # worked. Tracy # left.

Adjectives: Tracy # is tall. Tracy # is tired.

Identifiers: Tracy # is a friend. Tracy # is a lawyer.

Locations (in space): Tracy # is in the kitchen. Tracy # is in Paris.

Locations (in time): The party # is at 9:00 p.m. on Tuesday.

Any predicate that uses the vocabulary of a particular sensory mode is a clue to the speaker's preferences. The more frequently you hear someone use predicates from that sensory mode, especially when there's tension in the language environment, the more sure you can be that it's the preferred one.

The list below will give you a few examples of predicates from each of the sensory modes. Be prepared for a shortage of vocabulary in the smell and taste sets. Be prepared also for smell/taste overlaps; they mirror the situation in your body when your food tastes odd to you because you have a stuffy nose from a cold or an allergy.

SIGHT:

See, look, glance, observe, watch, appear, resemble, be clear, be transparent, be invisible, be foggy, be murky, see right through [X], have not even a glimmer of an idea about [X], clear everything up, have an eagle eye

HEARING:

Hear, listen, pay attention to what [X] says, be garbled, be full of static, be noisy, sound fine, sound stupid, be singing from the same page, sound like [X], talk [X] to death, be music to your ears

TOUCH:

Feel, touch, get, make, grasp, dig, handle, put your finger on [X], get hold of [X], be smooth as silk, be too hot to handle, be slippery, be easy to handle, get right down to business, be tickled by [X], be touched by what [X] did

SMELL

Smell, sniff, sniff around, stink, be rotten, be nosy, smell like [X], be where nothing smells right

TASTE:

Taste, gobble, be nasty, be sweet, be right on the tip of the tongue, make [X] nauseated, be sour, be enough to make [X] gag, be in a sickening situation

Now for the "translation" exercise. You don't have to be a fanatic about this. Perfect matches like the following set aren't common:

"That looks good to me."

"That sounds great to me."

"That feels fine to me."

"That smells right to me."

Notice that even for a simple and obvious set like that one we'd have to play around with the example to find a rough equivalent for the sensory mode of taste. We could say, "That leaves a good taste in my mouth," but "That tastes right to me" is not a likely sentence except if it's about something you eat or drink.

I'm going to give you ten sentences for practice that are hard enough to be a reasonable translation workout. By the time you finish them, you will have a good grasp of the technique. Here's an example set to get you started:

SIGHT:

"I don't think you should buy that car. I don't like the looks of the deal, and I don't like the looks of that salesman, either."

HEARING:

"I don't think you should buy that car. I don't like the sound of the deal, and I don't like the way that salesman talks, either."

TOUCH:

"I don't think you should buy that car. I have a funny feeling about the whole deal, including that salesman. He really gives me the creeps."

SMELL:

"I don't think you should buy that car. I think the whole deal smells fishy, and that salesman is a real stinker."

TASTE:

"I don't think you should buy that car. The whole deal leaves a bad taste in my mouth, and that salesman makes me sick to my stomach."

Practice Sentences For You To Work On

For each of these sentences, first identify the sensory mode that it's written in, and then "translate" it into as many of the other sensory modes as you can.

① "Maria has a good grasp of the problems involved in starting her own business."

② "When everything looks rosy, you need to be sure you're seeing things clearly."

③ "The mechanic said he wasn't sure he could do much about getting the car working, but he'd try hard to tackle it sometime today."

④ "All the team members understood what the coach was getting at, but they knew that following through on it would be tough."

⑤ "The president said we would all have to pull together if we wanted to get anywhere."

⑥ "I can't see things your way, but I don't think it's because you're not being clear—I think it's just that I have a very different point of view."

⑦ "Ellen said the trip sounded foolish and expensive to her, but if the whole family was going to sing from that same page, she wasn't going to argue."

⑧ "If you don't get hold of yourself, you're going to be in deep trouble."

⑨ "The weather was rotten, the people were rotten, and I could smell the lies ten feet away."

⑩ "Every time he says that word, it's like I just ate a tuna fish pizza cake with chocolate sauce."

You don't have to worry about knowing which sensory mode you're hearing; that skill is built into your mental grammar, and will be on automatic. What's new is the knowledge that paying attention to the sensory modes others are using, and matching them when that's possible, is a useful communication strategy.

Finally, if you can't easily match the sensory mode you're hearing, the fallback strategy is to use no sensory language at all. That way, you can avoid a sensory mode *mis*match. For example, if someone asks, "How bad does this problem look to you?" and "I don't see it as serious" doesn't come quickly to your mind, answer with "I don't think it's very serious." "Think" doesn't come from any of the sensory modes.

SYSTEMATIC ORGANIZATION OF UTTERANCES

Up until roughly the 1950s, what I am about to describe to you next was part of the education of anyone who went as far as the eighth grade. Nothing I'm about to say is new; it's material from the ancient rhetoric course and was ancient even when Plato was talking about it. Today, however, unless you enroll in a course on giving speeches or sermons, you're unlikely to learn much about the rhetoric of spoken language. Today's rhetoric classes are focused on teaching the use of *written* language.

We can't fit an entire rhetoric course into this book. But we can take up three techniques that are easily learned and that have a high charisma-boosting potential: parallelism, unifying metaphors, and culturally loaded vocabulary. They will make you sound as if you know what you're talking about, and they will give your speech a rhythm that is pleasant to the ear.

I once sat through a forty-minute talk by the most charismatic man I know, and I can assure you that it had almost no semantic content whatsoever. He had been scheduled to give a talk but hadn't bothered to prepare anything and was winging it all the way. When he finished, I expected some expression of anger from the audience; after all, they had paid to hear him. But it didn't happen. Everybody clapped, everybody smiled, and a woman in the row ahead of me turned around and said to me, "I didn't understand a word he said, but I just know it had to be important!" Amazing. That can only happen to people who have no training in verbal self-defense.

Parallelism

Charismatic speech is always balanced speech. That balance makes it easy to listen to and easy to remember. It makes following the speaker something you can do without effort, because you so quickly catch on to the patterns and know what to expect. The balance also creates that comforting—or stirring—rhythm I mentioned before, which most people can be counted on to respond to positively.

One of the easiest ways to work toward this balance is to be certain that whenever you talk about more than one of anything—and especially if you talk about more than two—you use the same language form for each item in the series. This is called *parallelism*. For example:

"I have a goal that will not be ignored. I have a plan that must not be forgotten. I have a vision that cannot be denied."

Now compare this with:

"I have a goal that will not be ignored. The plan that I've worked out is one that everybody has to remember. And my vision, now—just let them try to deny me *that*!"

You may have the feeling that the first version sounds pompous (it does) and is repetitive (it is), and that the second version is clear and forceful and makes the speaker sound like someone whose head is on straight. And you may be right. The version that is charismatic, however, the one most likely to provoke the "Let's march!" reaction rather than the "What a nice speech!" reaction, is the first of the two. Notice how carefully it is structured, with this pattern:

"**I have a** [one-syllable noun] **that** [modal auxiliary] **not be** [two-or-three-syllable past tense verb]."

Using *one* three-syllable verb ("forgotten") between the pair of two-syllable verbs ("ignored" and "denied") is the expert touch of slight variety that does not distract from the basic pattern but keeps it from being perceived as overdone. By the time the second sentence has gone by, the listener is relaxed and knows what to expect. So long as the pattern of parallel language forms is maintained, the perception of the speaker as charismatic will also be maintained—and content has very little to do with that. Politicians and expert trial lawyers know this very well, and they capitalize on it to the fullest extent. It takes much of the labor out of speaking in public.

One striking proof of this is the work of Donald Shields and John Cragan, two social scientists who programmed a computer to produce a nine-minute political speech that could be used anywhere, under any circumstances. The speeches written by that computer got standing ovations, time and time again. Which should, I hope, go far to dispel the idea that charisma is something you have to be born with.

You may never have to make a speech, in the formal sense of the word, although the ability to do so is well worth acquiring. It's very handy to have somebody around who can always be counted on to explain to the PTA, or the board of directors, or any other group, the content of some message that needs to be passed along. A person who can carry out this task without fuss and handle the audience in such a way that the listeners will always be in a pleasant frame of mind afterward, even if the message itself wasn't pleasant, is going to be considered *valuable*. It starts with "Jennifer, would you mind going down to Payroll and explaining that memo I e-mailed to them yesterday morning? The supervisor tells me they're upset about it, which means they didn't understand it." And it ends with Jennifer being sent to major conventions in luxurious hotels at her employer's expense, to represent the company on the speaker's platform. That's worth remembering.

But even if you have no interest whatever in formal speechmaking, the principle holds for ordinary daily conversation. All of the examples below are just plain talk, but all use parallelism.

① "I'm upset, I'm angry, and I'm annoyed." [*NOT* "I'm upset, and you've made me mad, and I am annoyed, too."]

② "Pick up your shoes, put away your socks, and turn off that television set." [*NOT* "Please pick your shoes up. And your socks don't belong there, they belong in the laundry basket. And you shouldn't be watching television."]

③ "Going to the lake would be fun, and going to the fair might be interesting—but going to see your grandmother would be appropriate." [*NOT* "It would be fun to go to the lake, and going to the fair might be interesting, but I think that going to see your grandmother is the appropriate thing to do."]

④ "If you're worried, say so. If you're scared, tell me. And if you're confused, explain why." [*NOT* "If you're worried, say so. Tell me if you're scared. And if I don't know what's confusing you, because you haven't explained that to me, how can I possibly help you?"]

⑤ "You can have steak for dinner—and no dessert. You can
have salad for dinner—and pie for dessert. Or you can have
half a steak for dinner—and melon for dessert. You decide."
[*NOT* "Look, you have to decide. Do you want steak for dinner? Fine, but then you can't have any dessert. You can
only have pie if you eat *just* salad for your dinner. Or I guess
you could have half a steak and then some melon, if you'd
rather do that."]

There is affirmative parallelism, as in "I will stay, and I will
work" and there is negative parallelism, as is "I won't stay and I
won't work" and—fancier—"I will neither stay nor will I work."
And if your head is beginning to have echoes in it along the lines
of "If nominated I will not run; if elected I will not serve," that's
fine. It means both that I am accomplishing what I set out to accomplish and that it is time for me to stop.

An excellent exercise for learning about parallelism would be
to go to a library (online or off), read three of John F. Kennedy's
famous speeches, and take them apart one sentence at a time,
noticing every parallel structure they contain. When you finish
doing that you'll know a great deal about parallelism.

Unifying metaphors

For a complicated plan to have any chance of succeeding, especially when there's opposition to it, two things are helpful: ①
superior force—the machine gun, the raise, the promotion, the
scholarship; or ② a unifying metaphor to use as a peg to hang
the plan on. Advertising agencies, public relations firms, and
image makers of all kinds rely on the second alternative. It's less
expensive, less intricate, and people don't dislike you for it afterward; furthermore, it tends to perpetuate itself. Unifying metaphors are essential to charismatic speech.

If we had to choose a single most familiar and popular Great American Unifying Metaphor, it would unquestionably be the Old West. That one can be used over and over again; it rarely fails. Almost every American has grown up watching Western movies and TV series; the whole elaborate system of the metaphor is something you can expect to be stored in almost everyone's memory. Whether any of it is true or logical or any of those good things is irrelevant. In the Old West, guns never ran out of bullets no matter how many times you fired them, all Native Americans spoke the same language and lived in teepees, and hired killers preferred horses to women. None of that has much logic behind it, none of it bears much resemblance to reality, but that doesn't interfere with the consensus perception of the Old West as having been that way. That metaphor is a perceptual peg, and a whole lot of things you don't ever have to mention are hanging from it just because they are presupposed by the metaphor. Such as:

(1) All cowboys were gallant and chaste and would have died rather than betray another cowboy.

(2) John Wayne is, was, and always will be the perfect man.

(3) All women who ran saloons were really Earth Mother types with hearts of gold, and if you had any problems, you could turn to them for help.

(4) There was always more of everything; you just moved on.

(5) Anybody in a black hat who wasn't a preacher was probably a bad guy.

(6) Doctors would ride thirty miles through a blizzard in the middle of the night to tend to you, and it was all right if you never paid them. The cross way they talked was just to cover up how tender and compassionate they really were.

⑦ Real men never cried.

⑧ No American ever cheated anybody or lied to anybody or stole anything except (a) those who were hung for it, and good riddance to them; and (b) those who spent the rest of their lives making it up to those they'd done wrong, and God bless *them*.

⑨ Real men didn't talk much, but they had deep thoughts.

⑩ The bad guys always lost.

And so on . . .

A construct like this is very useful. It saves vast amounts of time, effort, and money. If you can find a unifying metaphor to use as a peg for your proposal or your speech or your sermon, you can rely on all the presupposed chunks that go with it, and you won't have to go to the trouble of explaining them. People will feel comfortable with the things you say because they're already familiar with the metaphor; it's like a house they've lived in or a shoe they've worn, and they just *know* that you are someone they can follow with confidence. When John F. Kennedy organized the language of his presidency around the "New Frontier," he knew this, and the effect was predictable. The message was approximately "Follow me, and once again the bad guys will always lose, there will always be more of everything, real men won't talk much but will have deep thoughts . . ." and so on. He had no need to spell out all the details. Even if your plan is nothing more complex than getting fifteen people to the same picnic on time, a unifying metaphor is the handiest and most charismatic way to do it.

What you must watch out for, however, is a metaphor with presuppositions that not only won't help but will actually hold you back. For example, in 1978 California had a proposal on the ballot to do something about the problem of smoking in public.

According to all the polls, the proposal had good prospects for passing, despite all the money the tobacco industry spent opposing it. Even smokers, according to the polls, would welcome a solution to the nuisance of being glared at by people in restaurants, bars, and other public places. Logic was on the side of the proposal, as was common sense. But the measure was resoundingly whipped at the polls all the same.

There were a number of reasons for this, but a major one was the unifying metaphor that went with the proposal's slogan, which was "Clean Indoor Air." Who could possibly be against clean indoor air? Everybody. As a unifying metaphor it carries with it a list of presuppositions like this:

1. Nobody likes to clean house, but somebody has to do it, and it's probably you.

2. Air that is clean does not smell—have you changed your kitty litter, or not?

3. Air that is clean does not smell—have you run around your house spraying everything the way a decent person would, or not?

4. If you don't keep the air clean inside your house, your family will be embarrassed, and nobody will want to come have coffee or a beer at your place, and you'll be unpopular.

And so on . . .

That is, the decision was to choose between the Marlboro Man and the individual a friend of mine always referred to as Tommy Tidy Bowl. Once this metaphor had been drummed into the voters' minds for a while, no amount of money could have saved that proposal.

When you choose a unifying metaphor, be sure you know what its presuppositions are. In an emergency, it may be enough just to shout, "Wagons, HO!"

Culturally Loaded Vocabulary

The last of our charisma producers is closely related to the preceding one. Certain words and phrases are heavily loaded—either positively or negatively—within the cultural group that uses them. Small children learn at an amazingly early age that one sure way to get attention is to use one of the negative ones.

If you want to be perceived as charismatic, you need to know the culturally loaded vocabulary of the person(s) you are talking to, and whether those items have positive or negative value. Certain items will trigger positive presuppositions, others will trigger negative ones, and you need to know which is which. Some are overpoweringly obvious; no one needs to explain to you that you must be careful with ethnic terms, curses, endearments, and current media clichés.

Within any group that you're reasonably familiar with, your problems should be minor. You'll know what items are on the list, whether their values are positive or negative, and when to use which ones. When you're dealing with a group that's not familiar, however, you have to do some advance research—ideally, by discussing the matter with someone native to the group. (This process, known as "fieldwork," is a topic for experts, and won't be discussed further here. It will be obvious that you can't do it by sitting down with the informed person and saying, "By the way, I need to know which words and phrases are taboo in your group and which ones people really like to hear.")

A word that I've used several times in this book—"Anglo"—will serve us well as an example. In the United States, Anglo is an ethnic label roughly comparable to "Hispanic" or "Latino" or "African American" or a number of others that come readily to mind. Certainly it qualifies as a culturally loaded term. But does it have a positive or negative value in your speech? Let's look at a dialogue that will clarify matters somewhat.

EMPLOYER: "I've called you in, Bob, because I have a lot of re-spect for you and I think your advice could be a help to me right now."

BOB: "Well, I appreciate that. Anything I can do, any time. What's the problem?"

EMPLOYER: "It's something that just plain baffles me. I mean, we make it very clear how things are supposed to be run around here. There's a sign on the wall that says any employee more than three minutes late is sup-posed to report to the supervisor immediately. That's *clear*, right?"

BOB: "Sure."

EMPLOYER: "And they *know*—all of them—that if they're late they're going to get their pay docked for it, right? They *know* that."

BOB: "Yes, sir. They do."

EMPLOYER: "Then will you please explain just one thing to me, Bob: *Why* do they keep coming in late every day?"

BOB: "That's easy."

EMPLOYER: "I knew I could count on you, Bob."

BOB: "The problem, sir, is that we're Anglos and they're not."

EMPLOYER: [Long pause] *"What did you call me?"*

It's not that Bob shouldn't point out to his boss that the prob-lem comes from the fact that different ethnic groups have differ-ing perceptions and customs with regard to time. The problem is Bob's use of the word "Anglo." Bob may perceive both himself and his boss as Anglos, but the boss obviously does not share that perception, and hearing himself called an Anglo has offended him. There are a number of safe ways to provide the same message without using a term that might trigger a negative response. For example:

"The problem is that the American work ethic isn't part of everyone's cultural heritage."

Or:

"Sir, different groups of people have different ways of looking at time. I think that's what's causing the difficulty."

Either of these sentences might let Bob and his boss go on with the discussion and exchange some useful information. But the line "we're Anglos and they're not" may well be the end of all meaningful communication between these two men. Bob has no way of knowing in advance how his employer will react to the Anglo label, and would be wise to avoid it altogether. This is a tricky area once you get beyond the most simplistic examples. But the basic principles should be clear.

Suppose you're certain that a particular item has a positive value as culturally loaded vocabulary; then use it if you can, whenever it fits into what you're saying. This will set up a feeling in your audience that you are someone trustworthy. Avoid negatively loaded items. If you're at all uncertain about an item, leave it out of your speech completely. If you find yourself in trouble in spite of your care, and especially if you're not sure why, go immediately to Computer Mode, use the most neutral and abstract vocabulary you can, and maintain that stance until you have enough information to know how to proceed.

14

Special Chapter
for College Students

College students have special problems in verbal self-defense
that are not typical of many other groups. These problems
create situations which—if they appeared in a work of fiction—
would be rejected as too unbelievable. I can vouch for this personally: I spent twelve years as a college student myself, and
taught college students for years after I got my PhD, and those
unbelievable things do happen. Absolutely.

Your situation will differ depending on whether you attend a
small private school or a huge state university or are enrolled on
the Internet, whether you are a graduate student or undergradu-
ate, whether you're returning to school after a lengthy break or
going straight on to college from high school, whether you have
to work as well as go to school, whether you have some special
characteristic such as a disability or a native language other than
English, and more. Because covering all of these sets of circumstances in a single chapter is impossible, I'm going to try to speak
to a hypothetical "average" student. No such creature exists, of
course, but we'll make do.

I'm going to begin by going once more around the Verbal Attacks Octagon, specifically for the student, giving you examples from each section. These utterances are examples that should immediately alert you to the possibility of a confrontation if they were said to you. If you feel that you would be confused by any one of them or uncertain about how to handle it, please go back and review the chapter in this book that deals with that section of the Octagon.

SECTION A

"If you *really* wanted to pass this course, you'd write a *term* paper."

"If you *really* wanted to be accepted at this school, you wouldn't *dress* like that!"

"If you *really* wanted to get into this department, you'd retake the *entrance* exams."

SECTION B

"If you *really* wanted to graduate, you wouldn't be *interested* in going to parties."

"If you *really* cared about getting a student loan, you wouldn't *think* of walking in here looking like a thug!"

"If you *really* wanted to get into this sorority/fraternity, you wouldn't *want* to spend time with that Frasier person!"

SECTION C

"Don't you even *care* whether you get into a decent graduate school or not?"

"Don't you even *care* what your grade point average is going to be?"

"Don't you even *care* that the *rest of the class* has to sit and wait while I answer one question after another for *you*?"

SECTION D

"*Even* an *undergrad*uate should be thoroughly familiar with every *word* in the official catalogue of this institution!"

"Even a *chemistry* major should have *some* idea who Rimbaud was!"

"*Even* a student with problems like *yours* ought to know at least the *basic elements* of English grammar."

SECTION E

"*Everyone* under*stands* why you're having such a hard time keeping your *grades* high enough, you know."

"Everyone in this *class* understands *perf*ectly why you feel obligated to disrupt every single session with your ridiculous questions!"

"Everyone under*stands* why you always feel that you have to display your brilliance and make all the other students feel *inferior*, you know."

SECTION F

"A student who *really* wanted to do well in life would have better *sense* than to choose a dead-end major!"

"A student who is just not properly prepared to do college work really can't *expect* to pass at a topnotch school."

"A student whose outside obligations come before academic work really has no *business* being in college."

SECTION G

"*Why* don't you try—just once—to get your work in on *time*?"

"Why don't you behave like *other* students for a change and see what *happens?"*

"Why is it that *every* time I turn around you're *stand*ing there, waiting for me to make some special *arrange*ment on your behalf? Don't you *ever* think of *anybody* but your-self?"

SECTION H

"Some instructors would find it very hard to *believe* that a student with almost no grasp of the basics would have the gall to enroll in Advanced Composition."

"Some people in our class might think it was pretty *weird* if they saw a student shut himself up in the prof's office for hours at a time."

"Some parents would be deeply hurt if they spent twenty thousand dollars a year putting a kid through school and that kid couldn't even maintain a *C aver*age."

Remember, when you're trying to decide whether utterances coming at you are attacks or not, to follow these steps: listen for the emphatic stresses; identify the speaker's Satir Mode; and work out the presuppositions of the utterances. If you're not facing an attack—if the speaker is perhaps just very socially inept—don't respond defensively. If you do get involved in an attack and things don't go well, write down what happened and work through it. What did you do wrong? Sometimes the answer will be "Nothing." Sometimes you will simply be up against greater experience, greater knowledge or sophistication or strength, and you'll lose in spite of having done just what you should do. But work out what happened, and learn from it. If the person who trounced you is someone you're going to have to interact with often while you're at college, you need to put together strategies for dealing with the troublemaker in the future.

Identify people who can't be trusted. Instructors who say there won't be a final exam and then give one; staff who tell you that you've filled out a form properly and then not only bounce it back at you but charge you a late fee for doing it "right" the second time; students who borrow your notes or your books with a promise to return them and then don't. Such people are to be found on every campus. Getting taken in by them over and over again because they are *charismatic* liars, or because you can't be bothered to keep track of who they are, is poor strategy.

Now I have twelve rules—very basic and elementary rules— for you to use in your language interactions with faculty members at every level.

RULE ONE

Be *sure* that the instructor knows what name is attached to your face, and vice versa. You may think this is automatic; it's not. And it's critically important. When the instructor is filling in final grades and Student X has a point total that's right on the borderline between a C and a B, a decision has to be made: is there any reason to give Student X an extra point or two and bump the grade up to a B? If the instructor can't even remember who Student X is—which is not at all unlikely if he or she teaches one hundred or more students every term—no such reason will come to mind. It may not be fair, but it's human, like the instructor. Make a point, therefore, of going to the instructor's office at least once during the term, during regular office hours, and introducing yourself. Have a reasonable question to ask, if possible. If you truly can't think of anything to ask, just Level. Say: "I'm here to introduce myself." Do your best to be sure that you are recognized and will be remembered.

If you are the class superstar, this rule obviously doesn't

apply to you, and you don't need to take up the instructor's time. So often it's the straight-A students who *do* drop by, usually to ask if they ought to do an extra credit project.

RULE TWO

Eliminate from your language behavior, forever and ever, the mannerism that linguists call "Hedging." Typical Hedges look like these:

"I know this is probably a stupid question, but . . ."

"I'm sure everybody else except me knows the answer to this question, but . . ."

"I know I'm wasting your time asking this question, but . . ."

"I know this is against the rules and there's no point in even asking for an exception, but . . ."

"I know you said we couldn't turn in our papers late, but . . ."

"I know you probably already told us this, but . . ."

Utterances of this kind are exactly equivalent to wearing a big sign that says "Please attack me—I would love to be a target." Don't use them.

RULE THREE

When interacting with an instructor, never use any sequence of language, verbal or nonverbal, that carries the message "Okay, we're equals. No need to make any concessions for me, because I can do anything you can do." Instructors who aren't chronic bullies will have a rule that says you don't humiliate students in front of other people or make fools of them in ways that will fester and hurt. This rule is from the "Only Pick on People Your Own Size" Popular Wisdom collection. If you suspend this rule by making it absolutely clear to the instructor that so far as you're concerned you two are the same size (or you're bigger), then anything goes. And the chances of you winning the resulting encounters are about one in a hundred thousand. The instructor has all the power, and you cannot win, even when you are right.

If you break Rule Three you can of course forget all about Rule One for the instructor in question, because you *will* be remembered. Some students try to wiggle their way around Rule Three with Hedges. They say, "I know you're the one with the PhD in here, and I'm probably crazy to say what I'm about to say, but I'm sure that what you told us is not the accepted position on that matter within the discipline." Never use Hedges, period. And notice how strange that last Hedge is: It's straight Placating all the way up to "but I'm sure," and then switches to a vocabulary and style associated with academic Leveling. This move has no chance at all of working.

RULE FOUR

Be aware that if you have accepted an arrangement of some kind in a class or an office session and didn't protest it at that time, you are stuck with it. If you sat through the opening six weeks of class and never once asked what the grade would be based on, and the instructor announces in the seventh week that it's based on a final exam and four term papers and two oral presentations, *learn* from that. The faculty member is obligated to make that information clear very early in the course. If that obligation is ignored and everybody just sits there, the assumption is that you've all agreed to that arrangement. Complaining won't help; the instructor will add two more papers and a field trip, and you have not one toe to stand on. The time to raise objections to course requirements is in the first week, preferably in office hours. If you don't know what the requirements are (or what the office hours are), you can't do this very effectively.

RULE FIVE

When you are meeting with an instructor whom you're going to ask to do something for you—such as take you on for an independent study course, or write a letter of recommendation—take with you everything you can possibly prepare in advance and be ready to present it. If what you want is to have a letter written for you, have with you all the information that's needed, an addressed envelope with a stamp already on it, and anything else that might be useful. The fact that you tried to make the favor convenient is what counts, even if you didn't get the details exactly right. *Never* try any of the following:

> **"I want to do an independent study with you, and I came in to find out if you have any good ideas for one."**

> **"I want to do a term paper for extra credit, and I came by to see if you could suggest a good topic."**

> **"I know our papers are due tomorrow, so I thought I'd better come by and ask you for a couple of topics I could write on."**

> **"You don't remember me, but I took one of your classes three years ago and I can't find anybody else to ask for a letter of recommendation."**

Students do these things, and the results are never pretty. In justice to the helpless student who really and truly cannot think of a topic for the paper or the study and is not the sort of ignoramus he or she will be taken for if one of the sentences just listed is used to convey that message, here is what you *should* do. Go in and suggest a topic that is roughly related to what you're studying, even if you feel that the instructor may reject it. If that does happen, the instructor will almost certainly make an alternative suggestion, and you won't have made a fool of yourself.

There is always the remote possibility that your instructor will leap at the chance to do an independent study with you on French milk jugs in the Middle Ages, as you suggested. If that happens, your best move is to go ahead and do it. You will still be better off than you were when you had no topic, and you won't have broken any of the rules.

RULE SIX

If you behave like a doormat, expect to be stepped on and don't whine about it. Placating will get you stepped on. For example:

INSTRUCTOR: "How many pages of reading a week do you think would be reasonable for your project?"

STUDENT: "Oh, *I* don't know anything about *that*! *You're* the expert! *Whatever* you say will be *fine* with *me*!"

INSTRUCTOR: "I think two hundred pages a week should about cover it, then."

If this happens to you, remember: you asked for it.

RULE SEVEN

Before you alienate an instructor for a stupid reason—such as how great it would make you feel to demonstrate to the entire class that the instructor is wrong and you're right—remember this one thing: the day is almost certain to arrive when you will need to ask that instructor for something. A letter of recommendation. A job. An Incomplete grade. Permission to take an exam late. Something like that. When that day comes, the answer will probably be no.

I am not talking here about alienating an instructor for a good and sufficient reason. There *are* some of those—matters of principle, for which the consequences are a risk you take as an ethical position. That's a very different matter. There's nothing ethical about humiliating someone in public just to show off.

RULE EIGHT

Never let an instructor find out that you haven't read whatever it was that you were supposed to read, unless you've been asked directly and would have to lie to conceal that fact. (If you've let yourself be manipulated into a corner like that, you need to review your verbal self-defense skills and find out where the opening is.) This goes for the description of the course in the catalogue, the class syllabus and sheet of course requirements, the reading list, and so on, just as much as it does for the assigned readings. Ask a question *about* the item you haven't read; ask for clarification, explaining that you're not sure you understand. But for heaven's sake, if you failed to read something and are in trouble as a result, keep that to yourself.

RULE NINE

If you aren't sure whether you were ever given anything to read about some basic information item for a course or can't remember whether the instructor ever said anything about it in class, do not ask the instructor. Ask another student, preferably the class superstar mentioned previously.

It's unutterably absurd to go down in history in the instructor's memory as the student who, on the next to last day of the term, raised a hand and asked, "Is there a final exam in this class?"

RULE TEN

Never argue with an instructor in front of other students or other faculty or other *anybody*. (The only exception is the rare case in which it is genuinely a matter of principle.) Let's assume that the instructor *has* made an error of fact, and knows it, and that you have challenged him or her in front of the entire class, and you are right. You have now created a classic Cornered Carnivore Scenario, and if you are eaten alive you should not expect sympathy. There is no way to predict what an instructor caught in this kind of trap will do.

What can you do if you feel obligated to be sure that the rest of the students share your correct information instead of the instructor's misconceptions? This is an ideal opportunity for you to apply Rule One: Drop by the instructor's office and discuss the disputed information. You say, "You know, I read an article the other day that contradicted what you said to us this morning about the Beetlehopper Hypothesis, and now I'm confused. If you'd discuss it with me for a few minutes, so I can get it straightened out in my head, I'd appreciate it." The two of you are now alone; the instructor can admit the error if there is one, and will usually pass the correction on to the rest of the class. Properly, you should be credited when this happens; but if you aren't, the kind of nonverbal behavior necessary to get across to the other students that you knew it all along is not appropriate. If getting the credit matters to you, you can always brag about it later—not in class.

You will miss the glory of the big in-class duel, but the situation will have been set right with no loss of face to anyone. If this still doesn't work, and the instructor persists in teaching what you know to be false information—that's what counselors are for. Go talk it over with one.

RULE ELEVEN

Unless your instructor has specifically told you that it's okay, don't use any variety of NetSpeak when you're writing anything for the class, or even when you're *saying* something for the class. Not even LOL. Not even emoticons. No matter how frustrating it is to you to have to write out all those words and do without all of your favorite graphic things, just don't do it. It's one thing to fail a test because you don't know the answers to the questions; that happens to everybody once in a while. But failing because you couldn't bring yourself to write your answers in offline language is ridiculous. It may well be that as time goes by the language you use on the Net will replace the traditional variety, but that hasn't happened yet, and trying to hurry that revolution along is only going to cause you endless trouble.

RULE TWELVE

Sometimes, in spite of all your best efforts and intentions, you find yourself in a situation where you really *have* fouled things up. You are 100 percent in the wrong, you have no excuse to justify what you've done, and disaster approaches. Let's say, for example, that you enrolled in a class, went to it a couple of times, did none of the work, forgot to drop it before the deadline, and are therefore going to flunk. Or let's say that you challenged an instructor on some information and got nowhere trying to convince him or her that you were right; then you talked to a counselor, who got nowhere trying to convince you that you were wrong; then you spent quite a lot of time doing your duty by the other students in the class, telling them that the instructor is completely confused; and now, much too late, you have discovered that *you* are the one who's mistaken. Either of these will do as an example of impending academic doom.

In cases like these, there's only one thing you can do: Go to the instructor's office hour, sit down, and Level. Say that you're there because you're done whatever ridiculous thing you've done, that you already know you have no excuse for it, and that you have come in to clear it up as best you can. Do not rationalize; do not talk about how this would never have happened if it hadn't been for some other instructor's behavior; do not mention something the instructor you're talking to might have done to ward this off. Do not, in other words, try to spread your guilt around. Level, apologize sincerely, and be done with it.

Be certain you aren't Placating. There's a big difference between a Leveler's "What I did was stupid, and I'm sorry I did it, and that's why I'm here" and the Placater's "I *know* you won't have any respect for me ever *again* after the awful, terrible *thing* I did, and I don't *blame* you one *bit*, and I'm so ashamed that I'd go *kill* myself except I'm so stupid I'd probably do that wrong *too*, and if you threw me out of here this *minute* it would serve me *right!*" *Please* don't do that.

After you go in and Level about your mistake, any number of things may happen, and you'll have to deal with them on an individual basis. Again, that's why colleges have counselors; they're there to try to help you when you are in over your head. But first you have to follow Rule Twelve; any other strategy is only going to make things worse.

As you look over these rules, it may help to remember a few things that tend to get lost in the academic shuffle. One is that the whole situation is artificial. You are an adult, perhaps an adult with adult responsibilities, often an adult accustomed to giving orders and having them obeyed in at least one of your roles in life. At college you're suddenly in the position of a child again in many ways, subject to the sort of sudden whims and irrational incomprehensibilities you associated with grownups when you really *were* a child. I don't intend to try to explain to you what lies behind the absurdities you have to deal with, many of which will be blamed on "computer error." But keep firmly in mind that your situation, like childhood, is *temporary*. You will not be here, in what may seem to you less like a temple of learning than a vast mental hospital, for more than a specific number of years determined by your educational goals and your skill with the catalogue. On the day you're told that the twelve credits of French you were last year solemnly assured would allow you to graduate are no longer enough—you need three more credits—and that whoever told you twelve would be enough must have obtained that information from a document that contained "computer errors," say to yourself sternly: "This too shall pass. I do not have a life sentence at this place; I will be able to leave here and go on to other things."

If that doesn't do it, try shock therapy. Choose any disaster that does not apply to you, and say to yourself sternly: "I could have a *real* problem. I could have an incurable fatal disease. I could be on Death Row awaiting execution." Something of that kind. The point of this is to restore your sense of perspective, so that you don't have a nervous breakdown—you don't have *time* to have a nervous breakdown—and you don't assault an evaluations clerk over three French credits.

You must also remember that you are *normal*. That is, although the life of a college student may have been represented to you as a glorious series of wondrous events, the honest truth is that it very rarely is that way. If it's true for you, be grateful. You are greatly blessed. For the student who has just started and therefore knows nothing at all about most things, for the student who is nearing the end of the academic trek and therefore approaching the day when all the accumulated "computer" (and other) errors will suddenly loom up cumulatively like Mount Everest, the following situation is normal.

You are exhausted; you're stressed; you have headaches and colds and rashes and stomach upsets; you have no confidence in yourself; you have no idea what ever made you start this process, and you're certain that whatever it was, you were out of your mind; and in any case, it seems to you that you're out of your mind. If you can accept the fact that this is the typical internal state of the college student, and if you are not in need of professional help, most of that list will melt away. You'll look around you, you will talk to other students, you will ask faculty members young enough to remember being students, and you will find that there's nothing unique about your state. Everybody either feels that way, or did feel that way, as a student. And most students do make it through college and move on into the real world. *Talk* to a few people instead of listening only to your own internal repeating tape. And if indeed you do need professional help, if finding out that you are one of a vast crowd of people in your state of mind and body doesn't help, go get that professional help at once.

Finally, there is a mysterious phenomenon that will serve to finish off this chapter. I can only warn you about it, in the hope that foreknowledge will help you deal with it when you must. It applies primarily to graduate students and students in intensive preprofessional programs such as prelaw, premedicine, and the like. For reasons that I cannot hope to explain here, professors in these programs have usually developed a technique that is as insidious and subtle as time-release arsenic capsules. Some of them know they are doing it and are proud of it; others don't. Some do it because they consider it their duty to their students; others do it because their profs did it to them; others do it for no discernible reasons. Whatever the motivation, the effect on the student is the same, and it goes like this:

If you don't get an A in every course you take; if you don't get an A on every paper you write; if you don't get every prize and fellowship and grant you try for; if everything you submit for publication is not accepted; unless, in short, you are able to walk on water, you will feel a heavy burden of guilt. You will feel that you've failed your professors and let them down. **When you're enjoying yourself,**

no matter what you're doing or where you may be at the time, along comes the same burden of guilt—you will feel that you should not be enjoying yourself. If you were living up to what you owe your professor, you would be reading the professional literature or writing a paper or giving a talk. At this point, you stop enjoying yourself and might just as well give up and go write a paper, read an article, reread something you've already read . . . anything to relieve the guilt.

This state is achieved by verbal manipulation, on all channels, and is widely alleged to do the student good "in the long run." I can only let you know that it exists, that unless you are extremely lucky you'll have to face it someday, and that it will eventually fade away. The better prepared you are in the skills of verbal self-defense, the better your chances are of knowing how to deal with it.

15

Special Chapter
for Verbal Attackers

When I wrote the first edition of this book, this chapter's title was "Special Chapter: For Men," and it was followed by a chapter titled "Special Chapter: For Women." In those days, it really was the case that *outside the home* verbal attackers tended to be mostly male, and their targets tended to be mostly female. In the workplace, in doctor's offices, in politics and banking and sports and education and public life in general, most hostile language came from men and was addressed to women. At home, within the family and in intimate relationships, the situation was more balanced, with women often dishing out as much hostile language as men.

Today that has changed so drastically (especially in urban areas, and for the younger generations) that it's no longer appropriate for me to divide attackers and targets along gender lines. This doesn't mean that sexism has disappeared from our public culture. We only need to go back over the long list of blatantly sexist utterances about Senator Hillary Rodham Clinton that turned up during the most recent presidential primary campaign to see that it's still there. We only need to look at the wage gap between men and women doing the same work, at how few women run Fortune 500 companies, and at how few women are leaders in the hard-science professions, to see that it's still there. But the *public* language environment is very different today. I have therefore changed these two special chapters so that they're written for verbal attackers and verbal targets, no matter what their gender.

In my experience, verbal attackers who talk to me (or write to me) about verbal self-defense tend for the most part to be of only two types. The first type are the people who contact me specifically to explain, at length, how very wrong I am. It may be, they tell me, that there are a handful of individuals who make a habit of verbal bullying; after all, there are one or two rotten apples in any barrel. However, they tell me, such people are *rare*. Never in their lives, they assure me, have they ever carried out an act of verbal abuse, nor do they ever intend to. (And, they add, that's surprising, considering what they have to put up with.) "And," they ask me, "*don't* you even *care* about the terrible *consequences* of this nonsense you keep telling people?"

When these people are both sincere and self-aware, they have no new problems. They are confident and aggressive adults going about their business as usual. If instead of being sincere they are trying hard to convince themselves that what they're saying is true, then they have several new problems. One is the remodeling of that small portion of their self-image that has been jerked about, so that it will function the way it did before—confidently. Depending on how intelligent they are and what their principles are, this will vary in the amount of time and energy needed for getting it done. I suspect that the most common resolution is a brief self-dialogue like this one:

"Could I possibly be a verbal bully? Me? Me, the one who always remembers my mother's birthday? Me, the one who always goes to that school play the kids are in, no matter how stupid it is? Me, the one who never opens my mouth, no matter *how* many dumb things the rest of the team does to wreck our chances? Me, the one everybody knows you can count on in a crisis? *Me*? Naaaaaaaaaaah. Impossible."

Any number of aunts, grandmothers, fathers, neighbors, pets, friends, colleagues, houseplants, and more, can be fit into that dialogue, as appropriate.

When just one dialogue like that isn't enough, they may have to put in some time for a while keeping the walls up around the image. For example, when they suddenly hear themselves saying, "If you *really* wanted to . . ." and get an odd feeling that that ought to mean something to them, they'll have to lay on more mortar. And they will have to deal with the minor burden of having engaged in self-doubt, however briefly.

The second type are the people who are almost distraught, who tell me that for the first time in their lives they realize that they are verbal bullies, that they use hostile language all the time, that they are perhaps raising their children to be verbal bullies, too, and they want to know what the devil they are supposed to *do*, now that I've ruined their lives? Sometimes that's as far as it goes; they cut off their contact with me right there. And sometimes they stay longer; when they stay, we talk about the problem.

Because these people are now aware that they are chronic verbal attackers, they have to make a choice: Either to go on that way, knowing it, and live with what that will mean in their lives; or to change their ways, which they're afraid may be even more unpleasant. Their self-image still has to be considered, you see. For a man, there is still a very real worry that if he changes his language behavior he will somehow be *less* of a man. "Gentleman" is one thing in his vocabulary; "gentle man" may be quite another. For a woman, there's the worry that changing her language behavior would mean that she'll be seen—and treated—as a doormat.

And for both genders, there is the burden of guilt. All their lives they've been doing these things without realizing it—or worse, they realized it and were enjoying it—and they can't undo any of that now. There's no way to take it back. It's done.

All of these people, in both groups, face two questions. First, are they a verbal attacker, even a verbal bully, or not? How can they tell? Second, if the answer is yes, they are, then what—if anything—are they going to do about that and how are they going to go about it?

We can best begin tackling the first question by going around the Verbal Attacks Octagon, with examples. The question to ask yourself as you read these utterances is not "Do people ever say these things to me?" I'm sure they do. These are the kinds of hostile utterances everyone encounters in daily life. Instead, ask yourself whether these are utterances you yourself would use in speaking to *other* people; that's what you need to find out.

SECTION A

"If you *really* wanted me to get ahead, you'd make an *effort* to be polite to my friends, no matter *what* you think of them!"

"If you *really* wanted me to get through grad school, you wouldn't *always* be *nagging* me about *help*ing you out more around the *house*!"

"If you *really* cared anything about having a winning team, you wouldn't keep giving me *phony excuses* every time I remind you about practice!"

SECTION B

"If you *really* appreciated what I'm trying to do for you, you wouldn't *want* to sit around on the beach when you *ought* to be working."

"If you *really* had any consideration at all for your family, *you* wouldn't *want* to quit your job!"

"If you *really* meant for me to have a fair shake in this job, you wouldn't *want* me to be stuck off in a corner this way!"

SECTION C

"Don't you even *care* if this place always look like a tornado *just went through it*?"

"Don't you even *care* if your driving doubles our car insurance premiums?"

"Don't you even *care* if I don't get my fellowship just because you gave me one lousy C? Do you get a *kick* out of seeing me lose something I worked four years for, just because of *five* lousy *points* on *one test*?"

SECTION D

"Even a *child* ought to know that unless I go to this conference I won't get my *promo*tion! It's *not* exactly secret infor*ma*tion!"

"*Even* a *seven*-year-old should be able to understand that *money* doesn't grow on *trees*!"

"Even a *music* major ought to be able to get through algebra without pestering their *roommate* all the time, it seems to *me*!"

SECTION E

"*Every*body in this *house* understands why you're so impossible to get along with, darling . . . Don't worry about it."

"Everybody in this family under*stands* why you always spend every party sitting all by yourself—and we *sympa*thize. No kidding, we really do."

"Every faculty member in this department understands *per*fectly why most of the students who enroll in your classes drop out in the first two weeks, Dr. Jones."

SECTION F

"A person who cared anything at *all* about having a meaningful relationship would *know* that there has to be some give and take on *both* sides!"

"A boss who had any consideration at *all* for the welfare of the employees would stop and think what it's *like* to work in a place that's falling down around them!"

"A person whose salary is paid by the taxpayers should keep in mind that they're paid to *serve*, not to boss people *around*."

SECTION G

"*Why* can't you ever do *any*thing *right*?"

"*Why* don't you ever consider how the *things* you *say* sound to *other* people? Don't you ever *listen* to *yourself*?"

"*Why* are you *always* criticizing everything I do, instead of taking a good look at your *own* behavior? Answer me *that*!"

SECTION H

"*Some* people would never in a million *years* believe a story that was full of holes you could drive a truck through!"

> **"Some officers might be inclined to be a little *hard* on a driver who was having trouble staying in one lane."**

> **"Some parents might find it a little hard to *understand* why a kid big enough to have a driver's license can't find his way out to the *trash*."**

Well—is that you talking? And if it is, do you care? (Please notice that I am Leveling here. I'm not saying, *"Don't* you even *care?"* I'm just asking a neutral question.) We've now come to the second question: What to do about being a verbal attacker. If you don't care, the issue is closed, and that is your business, not mine.

Suppose, on the other hand, that you do care. You've read a lot of pages in this book on how to defend yourself against other people who say hostile things to you. Let's concentrate now on how you *stop* if it's the other way around. How do you throw out all those speech patterns that have been part of your language behavior for so long? And how do you do it without creating havoc in your life?

I will take it for granted that you've already thrown out all the overtly obvious hostile language behaviors like yelling at people, swearing at them, and calling them names. No more *"Listen,* stupid . . ."* and "Why don't you look where you're going, you *creep?"* and epithets like "Nerd!" and "Fool!" If you've been carrying on in this fashion, you have nothing to lose by giving it up, I assure you.

One thing that won't help is to keep the same patterns, with the same emphatic stresses, and throw in little verbal love pats here and there to soften the blows. That's hitting somebody with a stick and then kissing the bruise to make it better. For example:

> **"Sweetheart, you know I wouldn't hurt your feelings for anything in the *world*—you know how much I love you—but**

if you *really* **wanted me to get through school, you wouldn't** *always* **be** *nagging* **me about** *helping* **you out more around the** *house.*"

That's not an improvement. The sloppy stuff at the beginning makes it worse, not better, because it insults the intelligence of your listener.

Another thing that won't help is tacking a cancellation clause on at the end of the attack. First the utterance, then "and if that sounds like I'm trying to be *obnoxious* or something, I want you to know that I don't *mean* it that way." This, like "No offense, but . . . ," becomes incredibly obvious—and unconvincing—after the second or third time.

I have a radical suggestion to make: Just make up your mind that you will eliminate the patterns on the Octagon from your language behavior. Not overnight; that's impossible. (If you *were* able to do it overnight, you'd probably scare everybody who knows you.) Not without forgetting and having to start over many, many times. You're trying to break habits you've built up over years and years, and you're allowed to be human. What matters is for you to decide that those eight types of utterance are going to be absent from your speech from now on, and *mean* it. Every time you hear yourself use one of the patterns, *notice* what you're doing; pay attention to your language. If you've been using them twenty times a day and in the first month you cut that down to sixteen times, that's progress. You have your whole life ahead of you for making the change. The fact that the change process will inevitably be gradual is a piece of accidental good fortune; be grateful for it.

Another thing that will help is to use your journal. Take every one of those examples from the Octagon, assume that you want to get across the message it contains but you want to do it without being hostile, and work on it until you've found a satisfactory new way to express that chunk of meaning. For example, look at this Section H attack, and compare it with the revision that follows it.

> "*Some* **parents might find it a little hard to** *understand* **why a kid big enough to have a driver's license can't find his way out to the** *trash*."

> "**Son, I'm having a hard time understanding something. You have a driver's license, and you use my car. I understand that. I pay for the gas and the insurance, and I understand that, too. But when I ask you to take the trash out, I don't get any results. Those two things don't fit together very well in my head. How about explaining it to me?**"

The revised version is Leveling, and it should work far better than the original one. Just be sure you don't add any Popular Wisdom to it along the lines of "After all, if you expect to be granted privileges, you have to realize that with every privilege there also comes a responsibility." Your son will already have heard that so often that it has lost its meaning and will only undermine the impact of your message. Depending on his age and patience, you'll get one of the following back:

> "**Aw, you're** *always* **on my back!**"

> "**I guess I'm just a creep.** *Okay*?"

> "**All right, I won't drive your car any more.** *Okay*?"

> "**Maybe when I grow** up **I'll understand.**"

While you're throwing things out, you might also throw out all the proverbs and platitudes. (These are chunks of Popular Wisdom that have been given a rigid form, like "A stitch in time saves nine" and "Birds of a feather flock together.") They're useful only if you use them rarely and in situations for which they are the one and only most perfect response. If it's your regular practice to use either of these types of Popular Wisdom a lot, you may find it hard to give them up. I have a helpful trick for dealing with that. It's a line from author James Patterson that goes like this:

"You can't tell which way the train went by looking at the tracks."

As a verbal self-defense measure, this line is a useful response to anybody's fatuous remarks. The usual response is a silence, and then, depending on the generation your listener belongs to, one of these utterances: "You know, there may be a good deal of truth to that" or "You know, I never thought about it that way" or "That's *deep*." Every time you hear yourself spouting a platitude, add to it—unless you're in a situation where it would be unsafe or inappropriate to do so—"And furthermore, you can't tell which way the train went by looking at the tracks." This should break you of the habit, because it will draw your own attention to your behavior.

As a verbal self-defense measure, the train-tracks line is also useful because you can drop it into the middle of almost any argument on a topic that nobody involved really cares anything about—that is, any really *stupid* argument—and it will often bring a confrontation of that kind to a halt all by itself.

It will also be useful for you to have somebody's help in your project for change, if possible. Not somebody who'll jab you in the ribs every time and say, "Hey! You're doing it *again!*" in front of the whole world. Something more discreet is needed.

When I was a very young wife I found myself suddenly dumped into a social milieu for which I was completely unprepared and where I was terrified. What I did, in that state of panic, was adopt a manner so arrogant and so phony—complete with a fake British accent—that everyone present perceived me as intolerable. This did achieve one of my goals, which was to keep them away from me and let me huddle in a corner alone in peace. But it wasn't a productive strategy for me as a person, and it embarrassed my husband.

We worked out a tactic for heading off this sorry performance of mine. The moment my husband noticed me starting that behavior pattern or heard that phony accent, he would say something to me very softly—and he would call me "Margaret." It didn't embarrass me, and nobody else heard it, but it made me aware of what I was doing. There were evenings when he had to call me "Margaret" dozens of times. If you have a trustworthy friend available, the two of you can work out an unobtrusive code of that kind that will be a signal to you when your language behavior is turning hostile. It will help.

It will be obvious to you that your goal, particularly in those situations where you are the *dominant* person in the conversation, is to switch to Leveler Mode whenever that's possible. Often it will be neither safe nor appropriate, because you will be swimming among the sharks like everybody else. But it's essential that you always be able to work out what the Leveler equivalent for an utterance would be if your situation allowed you to use it.

And I promise you, if you do no more than throw out the eight attack patterns from the Octagon, the yelling and swearing and name-calling, and the Popular Wisdom platitudes, you will have decreased the amount of hostile language in your speech and writing by a tremendous amount. That's genuine progress, and it's something to be proud of. One of the effects it will have is that, to your amazement, other people around you will stop being so irritating all the time. (This is partly a matter of your perceptions and partly a manner of theirs.) You are using verbal self-defense strategies when you're not the dominant speaker, and doing your best to eliminate the abusive patterns when you *are*, and there's no way that those two factors in combination can fail to lower the tension in your language interactions very substantially. You'll run into people for whom it will do no good at all; that's inevitable. But you will notice a big improvement.

Last stop on the line is Guilt Station. What do you do about the problem of the guilt you feel? I have no instant solutions to offer, but I can tell you some things you must not do. You mustn't go on and on and on, either to yourself or to others, about what a monster you have been. That's useless and boring, and soon people will either start avoiding you or agreeing with you. On the other hand, if you really need to talk about this, if you wake up every morning with the problem on your mind and a session or two with a tolerant friend doesn't help, don't ignore that. Go to someone who knows how to deal with such problems (by which I do not necessarily mean your friendly and expensive neighborhood therapist). See a counselor. See a minister or a priest or a rabbi. Go to a crisis center or call a hotline. But don't ignore it. You should not be feeling a guilt that becomes an obsession, not once you've realized what the problem is and have begun working to change it. The time twenty years ago when you called the disabled child in your second-grade class "Creepy Crip" should not be haunting you now.

A certain amount of guilt is normal and has to be lived with and worked through. If you had been hitting people with a baseball bat all unawares and you were suddenly made to realize what you'd been doing and were persuaded to stop it, you would feel guilty. (If you *didn't* feel guilty, that would be worrisome.) As pain comes along to tell you to keep your finger off the stove, guilt comes along to remind you not to whack other people, physically or verbally. Expect it, deal with it, and do the best you can. That's all anyone has the right to ask of you.

16

Special Chapter
for Verbal Targets

If you suspect that you may be a verbal attacker, please read Chapter Fifteen. If, on the other hand, your problem is that you are often the *target* of hostile language and verbal attacks, stay with me.

The two most basic challenges you face when you're living with chronic verbal abuse, unless you are very unusual, are these: recognizing that this is your situation; and dealing with the guilt you are likely to feel when you defend yourself.

Both of these challenges are tied tightly to your self-image. It may seem as if it would be *obvious* to you that you are being verbally mistreated. But it's not that simple. It's not easy to accept the idea that you are someone who has been letting people abuse you verbally, and on a regular basis. How, precisely, did you—a person of intelligence and common sense and good taste—acquire the sort of worldview that would make you not only unaware that you were being mistreated but willing to put up with that as if it were a normal state of affairs? How are you supposed to deal with the idea that you've let yourself get used to that situation? How did you get this way?

For women, it starts in infancy. You are "Daddy's little sweetheart" and "Mommy's darling little baby girl." It goes with the nursery rhymes and the picture books, where the princes and pirates and even very small boys go off and have adventures, while women and girls sit at home, sewing fine seams and dining on strawberries, sugar, and cream. It goes with falling down and being picked up and cuddled, while you see your brother told sternly in the same circumstances that boys don't cry. It follows you into your elementary school reading books, where all the *important people doing important work* are male. In your spelling book the consonants are male, and they are reliable. The vowels are female, they can't be counted on for anything, and they get kicked around by the consonants. It follows you through high school and college, where all the important novels and symphonies and paintings and sculptures and poems and dramas and philosophies and scientific breakthroughs turn out to have been the work of men. It goes with you to church, where all things divine are male, and you gather generically in *fellow*ship while wishing goodwill to all *man*kind. The men at your workplace wear the same suit every day of the week and, for all you know, the same white shirt and the same pair of shoes; as long as their tie is different every few days, they've done their duty. You, on the other hand, are held to a very different standard. You are expected to look like a fashion model every single day, and there will be job-related penalties for failing to do that. Show any human frailty and you are "acting like a woman," which is bad; show no human frailty and you are "acting like a man, which is very unattractive in a woman."

It follows you into marriage, where you will probably do more than half of the housework and almost all of the caregiving. Manage a career and a home and your children and keep yourself "well preserved," and you will be greatly admired. Let any of that get away from you and you'll find that nobody is surprised, since that's what they expected all along. Nor will this improve as you grow older. In our culture, old men with any physical vitality at all are perceived as distinguished, their white hair and wrinkles admired as evidence of long experience and wisdom; old women— and their white hair and wrinkles—are considered profoundly unattractive. The highest compliment you can pay a new grandmother is still "You don't look *old* enough to be a grandmother!"

Enough? I hope so, because I am beginning to bore myself. But it is the truth. Things have certainly changed for the better since I wrote the first edition of this book in 1979, but there remains a bedrock of these outdated phenomena and perceptions that stubbornly resists all attempts to wear it away. And it affects all women, including women who consider themselves liberated, have advanced degrees, are successful in professions and trades traditionally considered the domain of men, and have never even *seen* an issue of *Modern Bride*.

It's harder to understand how men find themselves living with chronic verbal abuse, because most male children are still raised as if they had to grow up to be John Wayne. Often the reason a man becomes a verbal target is simply that he is a kind and easy-going person who doesn't enjoy verbal altercations. Sometimes it's because a man has grown up in a household run with an iron hand (and tongue) by a chronic verbal attacker and has never had any other model for his language behavior. However it happens, it is just as dangerous to men's health and well-being as it is to women's, and changing the situation for the better is very hard.

What is to be done about all this? First of all: *Pay attention to what's happening in your language environment.* Are you or are you not being subjected to chronic verbal abuse and hostile language? One time around the Verbal Attacks Octagon, with examples, should help. Do people say things like this to you, with emphatic stresses like the ones indicated?

SECTION A

"If you *really* cared about my feelings, you'd at least *try* to dress decently!"

"If you *really cared* about the kids' health, you wouldn't let them *have* all that junk food!"

"If you *really* wanted this project to succeed, *you'd* come in and do *mailing* labels on Saturday just like everybody *else!*"

SECTION B

"If you *really* understood what climate change is doing to this planet, *you* wouldn't *want* to join that group!"

"If you really *loved* me, you wouldn't *want* to take tennis lessons when you *know* I need the *car.*"

"If you *really* were interested in getting ahead, you'd *want* to go to a community college, which is where you be*long.*"

SECTION C

"Don't you even *care* if your mother is upstairs crying her eyes out because you're *breaking* her *heart?*"

"*Don't* you even *care* that we lost a *major* contract because you wouldn't work *over*time yesterday afternoon?"

"Don't you even *care* if your children all look like thugs because you let them wear their *pants* and their *under*wear *half*way *down* to their *knees?*"

SECTION D

"Even a *sophomore* should be able to write a paper that makes *sense!*"

"Even a person with no more concern for the feelings of others than you have should be able to under*stand* that we can't always have everything we *want* in this life!"

"Even a lawyer as *young* as *you* are should be able to understand that judges are entitled to res*pect* in their *own court-rooms.*"

SECTION E

"Every nurse on the *floor* knows what *your* problem is, my friend."

"Every member of this *club* knows why you feel o*bliged* to make us *all look fool*ish with your ridiculous *behav*ior."

"Everyone under*stands* that when people reach a certain age, they just aren't really *themselves* any more. Please don't worry about it."

SECTION F

"A *person* who wants to be treated with res*pect* should remember that respect has to be *earned* and *deserved.*"

"A person whose greatest pleasure in life is causing trouble and alienating people should not be *surprised* when they get *tired* of tolerating that kind of behavior."

"A person who can't even balance a *check*book would probably be better off *not* talking about choosing *insurance* policies."

SECTION G

"*Why* don't you even *try* to do something about the way that child plays her stereo? We have to *live* in this neighborhood, you know!"

"*Why* don't you ever pay attention to the *instructions* I give in class for doing the *home*work?"

"*Why* don't we ever go somewhere *different* for a change, sweetheart? I mean, there *have* to be *other* ways to spend an e*ve*ning!"

SECTION H

"*Some* people would find it a little hard to under*stand* why a person who's able to run a business can't ever manage to get to an *appoint*ment on time!"

"*Some* kids would think it was pretty *weird* if their parents wouldn't go to the PTA picnic."

"*Some* people would think it was really *strange* if they asked to spend a couple of days with a friend and got turned down just because of a *the*sis!"

If utterances like these are a constant feature of your language environment, you need to do something about that. The solution is not for you to learn how to use attacks like these against other people; you don't want to go from a situation where everyone describes you as "such a nice person" to one where you are perceived as a loose cannon and a bully. You need to aim at a middle ground between the two extremes. The fastest and most reliable way to get to that middle ground is to practice verbal self-defense as taught in this book, as carefully and thoroughly as you would practice any other skill, plus completely eliminating the attack patterns on the Octagon from your own verbal behavior.

The second issue—how do you handle the guilt you feel once you start defending yourself?—is more complicated. It will be harder for women than it is for men, because cultural specifications for women still tend to be focused on service, dedication, and never making waves. Many women have been trained all their lives in two ideas: if anything goes wrong, it's their fault; and their duty in life is to see that nothing ever goes wrong. For such women, realizing that they have defended themselves, and perhaps have done so in a way that will be remembered, may turn out to be a heavier burden than they had anticipated. Especially when the attacker is someone they love, who has always counted on them to follow the hostile language scripts for them and be their partner in verbal altercations, and who will resent being deprived of that comfortable state of affairs. Hearing someone who matters to you say things like "You used to be so much fun to be *around*, but you've *changed*, and I really want you to go back to being like you were *before*!" isn't pleasant.

The most important thing to remember for handling the guilt is that we now know chronic exposure to hostile language is as toxic for those who are attacking as it is for their targets. You aren't doing other people any favors—you aren't being kind or nurturing—when you help them go on using that sort of language and body language. The most helpful thing you can do for them is to stop providing them with the opportunity to do that.

It's a bit easier for men. Males in our culture learn very young that verbal confrontations are a necessary part of their careers and their public lives. They learn to admire the skilled verbal infighter, to keep track of the "one point for you, one point for me" scores as the confrontations go along, and they understand that the confrontations are a kind of sport; they don't take any of this sparring personally. (The man who doesn't learn this is the man who gets passed over again and again while other people, often less able than he is, are promoted over his head.)

Women, by contrast, are often puzzled when they see two men who have just spent twenty minutes trading vicious insults go off to lunch together as if nothing at all had happened. Men are equally baffled when they find that the woman they just went through the same process with won't go to lunch with them because she's angry. They perceive it as roughly equivalent to refusing to go to lunch with someone because you were just whipped at checkers. And when their "But you weren't supposed to take any of that personally, don't you *know that*?" is either not believed or considered to be insult piled on injury, they are reinforced in any negative beliefs they may already have had about women.

The fact that so many women (especially older women) are unable to play this game—and make no mistake about it, it is just that: a game—is one of the reasons there is still a "glass ceiling" in business and one of the reasons women are still making less money than men for doing the same work. Most men look upon verbal tussling much as they do any other sport: get in there and play to win, and then, after the final whistle blows, everybody go out together for pizza and beer. (Or steak and a good red wine, or doughnuts and coffee, depending.)

If you are a woman and you do not own the corporation, publishing firm, hospital, or whatever—which would change all the rules in a number of intricate ways—you need to learn to *understand* this game, even if it's not a game you're willing to play. People who go into a football game and insist on playing it by the rules of tennis are going to have a miserable time. They won't score any points, they're sure to lose, and other people will try to keep them from ever playing in their football games again. It's not a sensible strategy.

And don't ever forget that the rules of this game apply just as rigidly to the other women present as they do to the men. I have seen so many women who handle the confrontation game with casual ease in the typical team situation of one woman and seventeen men, but are completely disoriented when another woman joins the group. It's important to remember that the other woman isn't attacking you personally any more than the men are. Like you, she is simply playing the game as well as she can.

I have heard men say, with utter seriousness, "But it wasn't a lie at *all*—not in *that* situation." Whether it was true or not, they will explain solemnly, has nothing to do with whether it was a lie. On the football field, the man who pretends to be about to throw the ball to one person and then throws it to somebody else has not lied; it's just "the way the game is played." Women have to learn to anticipate this attitude about honesty and take it into account in planning verbal strategy. It's one thing to object to what a man says and understand that he said it because he perceives business as a game; it's quite another to object to what he says because you consider him a liar. And those two differing perceptions of the situation will have very different consequences for relationships and for communication.

Finally, I must note that this is another situation that is beginning to change. There are many women today who have grown up participating in verbal confrontation as a sport, are completely comfortable with it, and enjoy it as much as their male peers do. For them, this is no longer an issue.

There has been much research by linguists and other scientists on patterns of language allegedly linked with the biological gender of the speaker. This research has turned up some proposed characteristics of "women's language" that are claimed to be absent from "men's language," including the following:

① Intensifiers such as "very, extremely, really, terribly, totally, awfully"

② Tag questions, such as "I should leave, shouldn't I?" and "That's too loud, isn't it?"

③ A list of "feminine" vocabulary items such as "mauve," "teeny-weeny," and "simply darling"

④ Never being allowed to finish sentences, because of constant interruptions

⑤ Frequent use of "I feel" or "I feel like" to begin sentences

This research is useful, but some cautions are necessary. First, intonation and tone of voice are crucial to these alleged characteristics. I have heard very strong, masculine, thoroughly *male* males (in the stereotypical sense of the word "male") use every item on the women's-language list, including "teeny-weeny," without being perceived as effeminate or odd. There's a vast difference between saying "Mary is a simply darling person and I enjoy being with her," and saying "Mary is a *simply darling* person, and I just *love* being *with* her!"

Second, one reason women are more often heard and read using these items than the men they're being compared with is that the language characteristics listed are representative of the language behavior of *subordinate* individuals. Since women still fill the subordinate roles more frequently in mixed groups, the statistics that come out of the research will tend to support the hypothesis.

If the "women's language" concept for English is taken too seriously, there may be a tendency for women to try to cut the alleged "female" language items out of their speech and writing, and perhaps to adopt some of the alleged "male" language items. The idea is that this will cause them to be perceived as less subordinate, more confident, more competent, and so on. This isn't a good strategy; it leads to unnatural speech, and it's counterproductive. You only have to imagine a woman who is determined to interrupt as frequently as possible rather than allow herself to be interrupted, while the dominant individual or individuals in the confrontation continue to interrupt at their usual rate.

People who are verbal targets on a regular basis really can do a great deal to change that. They have to make a drastic change in their language behavior. They have to stop taking the bait verbal attackers dangle in front of them. They have to stop feeding the hostility loops that they find themselves dealing with. They have to learn to handle the guilt. As is true for verbal attackers, this isn't a change that has to be made quickly. It will take time, and there will be setbacks. But it *can* be done, and it will be worth it.

17

Emergency Techniques

This chapter is a collection of techniques to be used in emergency situations. With any luck, you'll never be involved in any of these emergencies, but one or two may come your way. I want to make it clear that what I offer you here are stopgap measures, and that some of the emergencies are more dire than others. If a surgeon tried to tell you over the phone how to do an emergency appendectomy, or a flight controller tried to talk you through landing a plane when the pilot had collapsed, neither one would try to fool you into believing that everything was perfectly all right. The techniques that follow are like those situations, except that only one can be called a matter of life and death. They're listed here in what I perceive as the order of their danger and their likelihood of occurring in your life. The most likely—and least dangerous—appear first.

WHAT TO DO WHEN YOU ENCOUNTER AN EXPERT IN VERBAL MANIPULATION WHO KNOWS WHAT YOU'RE DOING AND DOES IT RIGHT BACK AT YOU

It depends. If the two of you are alone, you probably have nothing to worry about. You'll go a round or two, perhaps have a good laugh, and then switch to Leveling; no harm done. Or else you, because you're a beginner, will be shown a trick or two, put in your place, and *then* the two of you will switch to Leveling; no serious harm done.

Unfortunately, this happens more often in public, in situations that may make it awkward for the other person to be gracious. In such a case, once you realize what you're up against, you have only one safe strategy—and even then, its safety will depend on the ethics of your opponent. Nevertheless, this is what you must do: rely on the expert to get both of you out of the dilemma safely. Go to Computer Mode and stay there; pay close attention to the clues the expert feeds you; don't betray by word or movement or expression any surprise you may feel at things that happen as the situation develops; and trust the expert's superior skill. Any attempt you make to "help" is likely to make it harder for him or her to carry out the necessary moves. Don't just do something, *sit* there. Quietly.

I went through a lot of unnecessary knocking about and loss of face as a beginner before I finally realized that my attempts to help the expert present were only creating problems and making things worse. I learned the hard way and would like to spare you that.

HOW TO HANDLE AN ANGRY GROUP

All the confrontations described in this book have included you and at most two or three other people. It does sometimes happen that you must face a really furious *group* of people, perhaps quite a large group. For instance, as a teacher you may have to face a room full of angry students or angry parents. As a speaker, you may have to face an outraged audience. As an officer of an organization, you may have to face a group of angry members.

First, let the group exhaust its anger if you can. You can take quite a lot of verbal garbage—the equivalent of thrown tomatoes and lemon pies—without allowing it to destroy your calm, if you make up your mind to do that. It must not be allowed to go on forever. And it must not be allowed to go on when it becomes clear that it's only feeding the flames. But in most cases, letting half a dozen people stand up in your audience and tell you what a mess you are and in how many ways you are that kind of mess, while you listen in polite and neutral silence, will lower the tension in the room and make everyone more willing to be reasonable.

When the half-dozen representatives of the group's anger have been heard and you have exhibited your willingness to let all sides of the question be aired, the next step is to behave precisely as if the group you face were only one person. This is not as strange as it may seem, since by this time a mob personality will usually have developed. It will be a Blamer Mob, a Placater Mob, or some other type. The only difference between such a mob and an individual is the ease with which the mob can be led—and the question is only whether you are going to lead it or somebody else is. Use everything you know about being charismatic. If things begin to heat up in spite of your efforts, switch to Computer Mode and be just as meaningless and abstract as you possibly can.

Above all, don't lose your temper or show any sign that you are distressed. An expert can Level with an angry group and get away with it, but novices are trampled into the earth that way. Don't try it unless it simply appeals to you as an experiment and you're willing to trade the consequences for the experience.

HOW TO HANDLE A SITTING DUCK

Every now and then you will face a moral dilemma—an ethical crisis. Somewhere in one of your language environments, at either your own level of status or slightly above it, there will be a pathetic example of someone you could easily take apart and make a pale gray smear of, verbally. Furthermore, this person will persist in begging to be treated that way, carrying out what Sitting Duck perceives as strikingly clever verbal moves against you, and waiting confidently for you to come back with *your* move and be carried away bleeding.

Once you spot this person, you have only one ethical choice, and it isn't pleasant: *Ignore* Sitting Duck. There is no honor, no victory, and no decency in using your superior strength and skill against someone of this kind, and you must not stoop to it no matter how tempting it is. Maintain Computer Mode, never lose your temper, and wait. In time, Sitting Duck will self-destruct, and it will be remembered that you never deviated from the proper ethical position. (By "in time," I really do mean "in time." It may take years.)

You will often be challenged about this by other people who will call what you're doing cowardice or hypocrisy or professional suicide or accuse you of "being a martyr." Some of these people will be well-meaning friends, and some will be pretending to be well-meaning friends; it makes no difference. You look them calmly in the eye, you tell them that you haven't the slightest idea what they're talking about, and you stick to that position. It is cheap and dishonorable to use your skills against attackers who can't defend themselves against you. Don't stoop to that, and the day will come when you'll be glad you didn't.

HOW TO HANDLE A TOTAL COMMUNICATION BREAKDOWN

Sometimes, nothing works. You say something, making all the proper moves, and nothing happens. You get an icy silence, a blank look, folded arms. You try another move—you try Leveling, perhaps. And still nothing happens.

What this means is that you are lacking some vital piece of information. You have broken a rule you know nothing about, perhaps because the other person is from a different cultural group than you are, perhaps for entirely personal reasons.

In this situation you have only one appropriate response: You become absolutely silent, too. And you wait. Somebody will break eventually and either say something or leave. You can hope that the somebody will not be you, or that the other person will offer you the missing information you need. If not, please remember— you cannot win them all.

If this happens to you in a situation in where you are facing a group and you have a responsibility to fulfill—for example, you're there to try to convince management that your union members are entitled to a higher wage, or to try to convince a faulty committee that a change should be made in an academic requirement—be sure that you make your position clear before you resort to silence. Say, unambiguously and neutrally, "What I'm here for is to talk about a wage increase. I'm willing to listen to what you have to say, and I'm willing to enter into a discussion." And then, *wait*. It's their move.

REVERSE-SIGNAL TECHNIQUE

What on earth do you do, as a novice, if you're asked to represent a position that you disagree with and you don't dare refuse?

This happens. In this real world, where people have families to feed and jobs to hold down and all sorts of legitimate pressures and threats hanging over them, this happens. Pretending that it doesn't, or that most people are capable of being saintly and standing by their principles regardless of the cost, is absurd.

Assume that you're a student teacher and you've been told to convince your students' parents that the book you're required to use in your classroom is a good one, although you yourself think it's a dreadful book. If you say you won't use it, you'll flunk student teaching, you won't get your teaching certificate, years of school at considerable sacrifice for you and your family will have been wasted, and somebody else will move in and do what you refused to do. That person *will* pass student teaching, get the teaching certificate, and move forward.

This is an awful moral dilemma, and I'm not here to hand down moral doctrine. Unlike the Sitting Duck situation, the issues are not clear cut. I once compromised in a situation like this, long ago, because I had small children to feed. I despise myself for it to this day; but if I had it to do over again, I'm certain that I would do the same thing I did then. It's not fair; you shouldn't be put in such a bind. But I assure you that when something unpleasant or unpopular has to be transmitted to a group, it's often a task that nobody high on the power hierarchy will touch; thus, it is "delegated" down the line until it arrives at you. The question then becomes: In a situation where you feel that you have no choice but to compromise your principles, is there any way you can do that without sacrificing the entire ball game?

Yes. There is a technique from espionage and advertising that you can use. It requires careful preparation, but is certainly not beyond your skills.

Write down what it is that you're expected to say—the part where you defend the book you despise, for example. Then consider your audience. Think of everything you know about them, their likes and dislikes, and especially what words or phrases might have a negative cultural loading for them. Make a list of those words, eliminating all swear words and epithets and open insults. Now go back to your speech and carefully salt those items through it wherever you can. Your goal is to make the audience ① leave convinced that they've heard you speak *for* the book you hate, since that's the compromise you have been forced into; and ② prepared to claim that they heard you speak in favor of it, but convinced that they hate that book. In other words, you have done your best and you have failed; that can happen to anyone.

I'm no longer likely to find myself in a position where I have to face a group of angry students and argue for a curriculum change that I disapprove of. However, that could very well have happened to me when I was still a college professor. In such a situation, I would have used this technique. On my campus, which was a huge urban multicultural campus with only about ten thousand parking spaces for at least fifty thousand people with cars, the parking problem was a Unifying Metaphor to end all unifying metaphors. It was a rare day when any student didn't have at least one negative experience due entirely to the shortage of parking spaces (and the lack of adequate public transportation). I would therefore have gotten up before the group of students and presented the curriculum change in speech patterns having to do with being at the wheel of a car, successfully negotiating the freeways and streets, finding a secure place to park, and so forth. I would have hammered away at the logical arguments *for* what I was against, since they're known to have little effect on listeners. And at the end, I believe the students would have gone out and voted down the curriculum change.

You might think this could backfire on you, and I suppose that's possible. You could overdo it to such an extent that it would become parody, but you'd have to work at it.

HOW TO IDENTIFY, AND DEAL WITH, A PHONY LEVELER

Earlier in this book I told you that there are probably no communicators more dangerous than Phony Levelers. They tempt you—seduce you, actually—into a position of total vulnerability. Then, whap! And it's too late.

The most obvious clues to identifying these persons are the eight attacks on the Octagon, with the emphatic stresses present but with a different vocabulary and style. The Phony Leveler will never come at you as any sort of overt and obvious menace. Here's a typical Phony Leveler utterance:

> **"If you *really* wanted to have a meaningful relationship, love, you would realize that it has to be based on a foundation of complete mutual *trust*."**

And a few more:

> **"Even someone as sensitive to others as *you* are should be able to realize how *pain*ful it is when you keep *secrets* from me."**

> **"*Some* people might think that because you refuse to participate in this discussion like the rest of us, you don't really *want* to be part of the group. You know what I mean?"**

> **"Look, I know you've probably been hurt so many times**

that you don't trust anybody any more. Everybody *here*, including me, understands that, and sympathizes. We really do. But a person who wants to get beyond the past and do some genuine growing toward the future has to be able to give up these old misconceptions."

Your tendency in response to such moves (which are made convincing primarily by body language) is to tell your secrets, lay bare your confidences, and *trust* the Phony Leveler—often in front of other people. Then, when it's too late, you find out that this is what it was all about, and now the phony has you right where he or she wants you. Phony Levelers will have a lot to say about how "paranoid" it is of you to be so "distrustful," so "unwilling to surrender your own preconceptions," and the like. Frankly, being frightened in an earthquake is not paranoid; it's common sense. Being frightened when you have a Phony Leveler after you is also common sense.

This is a situation where it's better to be safe than sorry. When you hear the Octagon patterns and you have a funny feeling that things aren't right, stay in Computer Mode until you are absolutely certain what's happening. Nobody can hurt you with language more deeply or permanently than a Phony Leveler. You are entitled to refuse to risk that.

VERBAL SELF-DEFENSE AGAINST PHYSICAL VIOLENCE

This is the last emergency scenario, and the worst. Let us hope that you never encounter it. With all my heart I hope that you are never a teacher facing an angry student who has pulled a knife on you, or a woman alone in a bedroom with a would-be rapist, or an elderly man facing a drunken thug in an alley. But I cannot guarantee it.

Trying to counter physical violence with verbal self-defense techniques is definitely not recommended for novices—but if you find yourself trapped in a physically dangerous situation and you must *do something*, here are my suggestions.

Go to Computer Mode and stay there. Many people determined to hurt you physically are as interested in seeing your fear and hearing you plead for mercy as they are in the violent act itself. If you show no emotion and don't appear to be either frightened or arrogant, you will keep them from achieving that goal. This may win you some time, while they keep trying to get you to show the terror they want to see. It may be enough time for someone to come to your aid. It might also convince the attacker to find somebody who is more fun to abuse than you are.

Your goal is to keep the level of tension low, to keep your *attacker* from panicking—a major danger, however strange it may seem—and to win time. Be as absolutely neutral as you possibly can. Do not Blame. Do not Placate, whatever you do. Do not let yourself fall into Distracter Mode, which betrays inner panic. Stay in Computer Mode, verbally and nonverbally.

In the hands of an expert, this will usually work. That is why experts are sent to negotiate with persons who've shut themselves up in buildings with hostages at gunpoint. That's why experts are sent to try to talk people down from ledges and bridge railings when they are determined on suicide. In a beginner's hands it may fail, but it is worth a try. It is most assuredly safer than an attempt at physical violence, unless you are an expert at one of the physical martial arts.

Do your very best to get your attacker involved in an abstract discussion of violence—not the particular altercation the two of you are caught in, but violence in general—using Computer Mode as much as possible. The longer you can keep the potentially violent person talking to you, the better your chances of coming out of the episode without serious injury.

I am convinced that unless you *are* an expert in a physical martial art and capable of using it to defend yourself, this is much safer than the frequently recommended pepper spray, jabs to the eyes or groin, tasers, and the like. If you make a mistake with one of *those,* you're not likely to get a second chance. Just talking, on the other hand, is less likely to be interpreted as an attack or to panic the violent person you are dealing with.

Good luck to you.

18

Verbal Self-Defense
in E-Language

When I wrote the first edition of this book, there was no need for information about dealing with e-language—language from blogging, texting, twittering, listservs, forums, e-mail, video gaming, sites like MySpace and Facebook and Second Life, and more. Today, hostile e-language (commonly called "cyberbullying") is a serious problem, estimated to involve at least a third of our young people and many adults as well. That problem now requires its own version of verbal self-defense. Here are the four basic principles from Chapter 1 applied to e-language.

FIRST PRINCIPLE:
KNOW THAT YOU ARE UNDER ATTACK

It's harder, in e-language, to be sure that you're under attack. In spoken language, even on the telephone, you have intonation and tone of voice to help you sort out and interpret the emotional messages; face-to-face, you have facial expressions and gestures and other body language. E-language brings with it none of those things. Remember that in English the emotional messages are carried mostly by the body language, which can cancel the literal meaning of the words you say and hear (or sign and see).

However, that's well-known information; anybody who is fluent in spoken English is well aware of the fact that "it's not what you say, it's how you say it." For that reason, I think it's reasonable for your default position to be an assumption that *primitive* hostile e-language—obscenities, cursing, open name-calling, ethnic slurs, and the like—is intended to be hostile. Unless you have reason to believe that the person you're interacting with is totally new to the e-language environment, that's also true for e-language written entirely in capital letters.

Beyond that primitive level, however, it gets very hard to be sure that e-language coming at you is hostile. Every English VAP has an associated utterance that uses the same words, set to a quite different tune, that is *not* an attack. The question "Why do you spend so much of your time playing video games?" isn't an attack. It may be very rude or inappropriate or klutzy, depending on the relationships the people involved have with one another, but it's not an attack. It's just a request for information. "WHY do you spend SO MUCH of your TIME playing VIDEO games?!" on the other hand, is an attack. The only difference between those two sequences is the tunes the words are set to, and any other body language that might come with them. *That information isn't available to you in e-language.* You have to figure out the emotional message without it, from such things as the context, what (if anything) you know about the person writing and other equally vague factors. In a medium where you may not even know the *identity* of the person writing the language, that's a real challenge.

It's easy to say, "Oh well . . . when somebody posts a comment telling you that what you've just posted is the most stupid and ignorant thing they've ever read, it doesn't take a giant intellect to recognize that it's hostile." However, in face to face communication I could say "What you just said is the stupidest and most ignorant thing I've ever heard," or any other insulting sequence you care to propose, and still say it in such a way that you would know I really was not being hostile.

Your best move is to avoid leaping to conclusions. Start by assuming that the language isn't hostile unless you have good reasons to think that it is. Respond neutrally, and see what happens. Like this:

DIALOGUE 1:

>   X: "Why do you spend so much of your time playing video games?"
>
> YOU: "I really enjoy it. It's what I like to do."
>
>   X: "Oh. Okay."

DIALOGUE 2:

>   X: "Why do you spend so much of your time playing video games?"
>
> YOU: "I'd rather not answer that question."
>
>   X: "Oh. Sorry."

DIALOGUE 3:

>   X: "Why do you spend so much of your time playing video games?"
>
> YOU: "I really enjoy it. It's what I like to do."
>
>   X: "Well, that just shows how stupid you are."

DIALOGUE 4:

>   X: "Why do you spend so much of your time playing video games?"

YOU: "I'd rather not answer that question."

X: "Really. Well, I'd rather you DID answer it. Let's try this again. WHY do you spend so much of your time playing video games?"

If the interaction goes as in dialogue 1 or 2, you know you're just dealing with somebody who's Leveling. You've Leveled back, and that's the end of it; the question wasn't intended as an attack. If it goes as in 3 or 4, however, that's different; you *are* under attack.

SECOND PRINCIPLE: KNOW WHAT KIND OF ATTACK YOU ARE FACING

When the attack is one of the primitive kinds, you'll know it immediately. Beyond that level, you have to base your judgment on such things as the sophistication of the e-language and the number of moves that are made before the hostility becomes obvious. In dialogues 3 and 4 above, where the writer already shows obvious hostility in only the second move, you probably aren't facing much skill. But in this example, things are different:

DIALOGUE 5:

X: "Why do you spend so much of your time playing video games?"

YOU: "I really enjoy it. It's what I like to do."

X: "A lot of people feel that way."

YOU: "Right. When we have some spare time, that's what we prefer to do with it."

X: "Even if you never get out of the house."

YOU: "Hey, to us it *is* getting out of the house."

X: "Well, that just shows how stupid you are."

This time, X played along for a while, pretending to be interested in having a conversation, and only switched to the "gotcha!" line at the fourth move. That shows more skill. Someone who can write whole paragraphs of pretended conversation, perhaps getting you genuinely interested, is even more skilled, and may be a formidable opponent.

THIRD PRINCIPLE: KNOW HOW TO MAKE YOUR DEFENSE FIT THE ATTACK

When what you're up against is the primitive attack, the defense that fits the attack is simple: you don't respond at all. When the attack isn't primitive, the thing to do is to respond just as you would in speech, using everything you have learned about verbal self-defense. Follow the same rules for using the Satir Modes and the Sensory Modes that you would use in spoken interactions; follow the same rules for responding to VAPs. Don't set up hostility loops; don't feed hostility loops set up by other people. Use only as much verbal force as is genuinely necessary. Do everything you can to reduce tension in the interaction. Do everything you can to preserve face for everyone involved. Never *reward* hostile e-language. *Do not feed the troll.*

One thing that's different in applying this principle online is the fact that you may decide that you aren't going to respond, even when the attack can't be described as primitive. This is exactly like refusing to respond to speech in the real world, and in our culture answering someone only with silence is itself considered hostile. There are times when that's appropriate, just as refusing to participate in a shouting match offline is appropriate. Just be sure that when you decide that you're going to do that, you *stick* to it. No matter how many more emails (or other e-language items) your attacker sends you, and no matter how infuriating they are, maintain your silence. Otherwise, the message you're sending is that if an attacker just hangs in there long enough, you will respond. That's not a message you want to send.

FOURTH PRINCIPLE:
KNOW HOW TO FOLLOW THROUGH

In e-language, the hardest part of following through is almost always just resisting the temptation to *participate* in hostile interactions. Remember: the cyberbully's goal is (1) to get your attention, (2) to provoke you into showing as much emotion with that attention as possible, and (3) to demonstrate the power to *hold* your attention by keeping you trapped in the interaction for as long as possible. Those three things are the rewards—the payoff—for e-language attack.

And there's more. At first glance, it seems puzzling that those rewards are so attractive. In offline bullying, the bully gets to actually see and hear the effects of the hostile language. The targeted person may cry or plead or panic or scream insults or run away. Other people who are standing around get to observe all this physical proof of the bully's power over the target. In e-language that proof isn't nearly as vivid.

But e-language is a permanent record. Even when you've done everything you can to delete it, you never know whether, and where, and by whom, it was copied before you could do that. Cyberbullies can spend endless time reading and rereading the records of their hostile interactions—wallowing in them, admiring their own performance, enjoying their own cleverness, enjoying their targets' reactions as the bullies choose to interpret them, reliving the experience over and over again. This isn't an opportunity that bullies who use only speech ever have available, and it adds a great deal of extra satisfaction to an attack. When you give in to the temptation to provide those rewards, the cyberbully wins, no matter what else happens. Knowing that should help you resist the temptation.

The payoff for cyberbullies is simply *power*—the satisfaction that they get from feeling that they have the power to tie up other people's time and energy with their hostile words. Their targets have plans for how they're going to spend their next thirty minutes or so. But along comes the bully with the hostile language, and the target takes the bait and spends those thirty minutes fighting with the bully. Cyberbullies can hijack their targets' time and energy and sabotage their plans, often in front of a very large audience. That feeling of power is enough reward to make cyberbullying worthwhile to those who practice it, even without the target's angry or frightened intonation and facial expression, without the yelling and crying, without the flushed faces, without the shaking . . . even without all those physical goodies that—in spoken language—serve as evidence of the bully's power.

WHEN DO YOU HAVE TO BRING IN OUTSIDE AUTHORITIES?

When does hostile e-language reach a point where self-defense is no longer enough? When does it become necessary for outside authorities—for example, service providers, or law enforcement personnel—to be brought in?

Exactly as with spoken language, you need outside assistance when the danger becomes physical. When the hostile language is about doing physical harm and damage in the outside world. Anything that you can do to keep things from reaching that level, anything you can do to keep the hostility from escalating from verbal violence to physical violence, is a victory.

"LISTENING" IN E-LANGUAGE

Offline, there's a very important rule called Miller's Law:

"In order to understand what another person is saying, you must assume it is true and try to imagine what it could be true of."

Which means that the proper response when somebody tells you their toaster has been talking to them is to ask "What has your toaster been saying?" and then to *listen with your total attention,* so that you will have the information for trying to imagine what it could be true of. In e-language you can ask the question—but listening with your total attention isn't possible. It seems to me, however, that the e-language translation for Miller's Law is this:

"Instead of posting in haste, take great care."

Which means:

① Read the item *all the way through,* from beginning to end, before you respond to it.

② Read your response to the item all the way through from beginning to end before you send it.

③ If you're uneasy about your response, read it *out loud* (if you're somewhere where that's possible), listening carefully to your own intonation and tone of voice before you send it. If what you hear sounds snarky to you, fix that before you send it. If you're not somewhere where you can do that, do it "in your head" as well as you can.

④ Then wait a while. Wait an hour; if emotions seem to be running high, wait twenty-four hours.

⑤ Go back and read both the item and your response again, all the way through from beginning to end. And then, if you're satisfied, send your message.

What makes careless e-language so dangerous is the combination of ① the speed with which you can send e-language on its way, ② the absence of all the emotional clues that help us understand spoken language, and ③ the fact that all e-language has to be considered a permanent record.

LEAD BY EXAMPLE

You can't control the e-language that comes your way, but you do have the power to set up and maintain a nonhostile language environment in the e-language that you send and publish. The more firmly committed you are to refusing to either use hostile e-language yourself or respond to others' hostile e-language with hostility in return, the more likely it is that cyberbullies will avoid you.

References & Suggested Readings

[Note: Internet addresses often change with time. If you try one below and it doesn't work, please go to http://www.google.com and type the title and author of the item into the search box on the screen. Most of the time that will let you find the current address.]

Articles

Blanck, P.D. "What Empirical Research Tells Us: Studying Judges' and Juries' Behavior." *The American University Law Review* 40 (1991): 775-804.

———. "Off the Record: Nonverbal Communication in the Courtroom." *Stanford Lawyer,* Spring 1987: 18–23, 39.

Blanck, P.D., et al. "The Appearance of Justice: Judges' Verbal and Nonverbal Behavior in Criminal Jury Trials." *Stanford Law Review,* November 1985: 89–163.

Bohannon, L. "Shakespeare in the Bush." *Natural History,* August–September 1966: 28–33. http://www.cc.gatech.edu/home/idris/Essays/Shakes_in_Bush. htm/. This classic article is a fine demonstration of the astonishing communication breakdowns that can happen when speakers don't share the same basic presuppositions.

Boyle, S.H., R.B. Williams, D.B. Mark, et al. "Hostility as a Predictor of Survival in Patients With Coronary Artery Disease." *Personality Psychosomatic Medicine* 66 (2004):629–632. http://www.psychosomaticmedicine.org/cgi/ content/full/66/5/629. The Internet version of this article includes a long list of links to related online materials.

Cohn, C. "Slick'ems, Glick'ems, Christmas Trees, and Cookie Cutters: Nuclear Language and How We Learned to Pat the Bomb." *Bulletin of the Atomic Scientists,* June 1987: 17–24.

Cosmides, L. "Invariance in the Acoustic Expression of Emotion During Speech." *Journal of Experimental Psychology,* December 1982: 864–881.

Dickerson, D. "Cyberbullies on Campus." http://law.utoledo.edu/students/ lawreview/volumes/v37n1/Dickerson.htm.

Ekman, P. and W.V. Friesen. "Nonverbal Leakage and Clues to Deception." *Psychiatry* 32 (1969): 88–106. Links to many more articles and book chapters through 2006 by Ekman and his associates are available at http://www.paulekman.com/.

Elgin, S.H. "How Verbal Self-Defense Works." http://people.howstuffworks.com/vsd.htm.

Engst, A.C. "Confessions of a Twitter Convert." http://db.tidbits.com/article/9228.

Hall, E. "Giving Away Psychology in the 80's: George Miller interviewed by Elizabeth Hall." *Psychology Today,* January 1980: 38–50 and 97–98. This interview is the source for "Miller's Law."

Jackson, B., et al. "Does Harboring Hostility Hurt? Associations Between Hostility and Pulmonary Function in the Coronary Artery Risk Development in (Young) Adults (CARDIA) Study." *Journal of Health Psychology* 26 (2007): 3;333–340. [http://www.apa.org/journals/releases/hea263333.pdf.]

Jones, E.E. "Interpreting Interpersonal Behavior: The Effects of Expectancies." *Science* for October 3, 1986: 41–46.

Koop, C. E., and G.D. Lundley. "Violence in America: A Public Health Emergency." *Journal of the American Medical Association (JAMA),* June 10, 1992: 3075–76. The entire journal is a special issue on this topic.

Lenhart, A., et al. "Teens and Social Media." http://www.pewinternet.org/PPF/r/230/report_display.asp.

McConnell-Ginet, S. "Intonation in a Man's World." In *Language, Gender and Society,* eds. B. Thorne et al. 69–88. Rowley, MA: Newbury House, 1983.

Moran, T.P. "Public Doublespeak: 1984 and Beyond." *College English* 37:2 (October 1975): 200–222.

Munro, Kali. "Conflict in Cyberspace: How to Resolve Conflict Online." http://www.kalimunro.com/article_conflict_online.html.

Reingold, J., and J.L. Yang. "The Hidden Workplace." *Fortune*, July 23, 2007: 98–106. http://money.cnn.com/magazines/fortune/fortune_archive/2007/07/23/100135706/index.htm

Seligman, J., et al. "The Wounds of Words: When Verbal Abuse Is Scary As Physical Abuse." *Newsweek*, October 12, 1992: 90–92.

Sontag, S. "The Double Standard of Aging." *Saturday Review*, September 23, 1972: 29–38.

Williams, R.B., J.C. Barefoot, and N. Schneiderman. "Psychosocial Risk Factors for Cardiovascular Disease: More Than One Culprit at Work." *JAMA* 290 (2003): 2190–2192. http://tinyurl.com/2ce3hh. The Internet version of this article includes a long list of links to related online materials.]

Books

Birdwhistell, R.L. *Kinesics and Context: Essays on Body Motion Communication.* Philadelphia: University of Pennsylvania Press, 1970.

Bolinger, D. *Intonation and Its Parts: Melody in Spoken English.* Palo Alto, CA: Stanford University Press, 1986.

Bolton, E. *People Skills: How to Assert Yourself, Listen to Others and Resolve Conflicts.* Englewood Cliffs, NJ: Prentice Hall, 1979.

Crystal, D. *Language and the Internet.* Cambridge: Cambridge University Press, 2006.

Elgin, S.H. *The Gentle Art of Verbal Self-Defense at Work.* Paramus, NJ: Prentice Hall Press/Penguin, 2000.

———. *Peacetalk 101.* Maple Shade, NJ: Lethe Press, 2000.

———. *How To Disagree Without Being Disagreeable*. New York: John Wiley & Sons, 1997.

———. *The Gentle Art of Communicating with Kids*. New York: John Wiley & Sons, 1996.

———. *You Can't Say That To Me!: Ending the Pain of Verbal Abuse*. New York: John Wiley & Sons, 1995.

———. *GenderSpeak: Men, Women, and the Gentle Art of Verbal Self-Defense*. New York: John Wiley & Sons, 1993.

Everstine, D.S., and L. Everstine. *People in Crisis: Strategic Therapeutic Interventions*. New York: Brunner/Magel, 1983.

Fisher, R. and W. Ury. *Getting to Yes: Negotiating Agreement Without Giving In*. New York: Penguin, 1983.

Goleman, D. *Emotional Intelligence*. New York: Bantam, 1995.

Goleman, D. and J. Gurin, eds. *Mind*Body Medicine*. Yonkers, New York: Consumer Reports Books, 1993.

Gordon, T. *Leader Effectiveness Training: L.E.T.* New York: Wyden Books, 1977.

Grinder, J. and R. Bandler. *The Structure of Magic*, Vol. 2. Palo Alto, CA: Science and Behavior Books, Inc., 1976. See especially 3–26.

Hall, E.T. *Beyond Culture*. New York: Doubleday/Anchor, 1977.

———. *The Silent Language*. New York: Doubleday/Anchor, 1959.

Lakoff, G. and M. Johnson. *Metaphors We Live By*. Chicago: University of Chicago Press, 1980.

Lakoff, R. *Language and Woman's Place*. New York: Harper & Row, 1975. This brief book is one of the landmark publications in the literature on characteristics of women's language.

Lynch, J.J. *The Language of the Heart: The Body's Response to Human Dialogue*. New York: Basic Books, 1985.

———. *The Broken Heart: The Medical Consequences of Loneliness*. New York: Basic Books, 1977.

Nierenberg, G.I. and H.H. Calero. *How to Read a Person Like a Book*. New York: Pocket Books, 1971. This is a typical example of a popular treatment of the subject of body language.

Satir, Virginia. *Peoplemaking.* Palo Alto, CA: Science and Behavior Books, Inc., 1972.

———. *Conjoint Family Therapy.* Palo Alto, CA: Science and Behavior Books, Inc., 1964.

Tannen, D. *You Just Don't Understand: Women and Men in Conversation.* New York: William Morrow, 1990.

Wilkins, F. *Persuasive Jury Communication: Case Studies from Successful Trials.* Colorado Springs. CO: Shepard's/McGraw-Hill, 1994.

Williams, R.B. and V. Williams. *Anger Kills: Seventeen Strategies for Controlling the Hostility That Can Harm Your Health*. New York: Harper, 1993.

Index